YORK FILM NOTES

The Third Man

Director
Carol Reed

Note by John Hoare

Longman  York Press

York Press
322 Old Brompton Road, London SW5 9JH

Pearson Education Limited
Edinburgh Gate, Harlow, Essex CM20 2JE, United Kingdom
Associated companies, branches and representatives throughout
the world

© Librairie du Liban *Publishers* and Pearson Education Limited 2000

All rights reserved. No part of this publication may be reproduced, stored in a retrieval system, or
transmitted in any form or by any means, electronic, mechanical, photocopying, recording, or
otherwise, without either the prior written permission of the Publishers or a licence permitting
restricted copying in the United Kingdom issued by the Copyright Licensing Agency Ltd,
90 Tottenham Court Road, London W1P 9HE

Screenplay and stills © Canal+ Image UK Ltd

First published 2000

ISBN 0-582-40511-4

Designed by Vicki Pacey
Phototypeset by Gem Graphics, Trenance, Mawgan Porth, Cornwall
Colour reproduction and film output by Spectrum Colour
Printed in Malaysia, KVP

contents

background 5
trailer 5
reading the third man 7
key players' biographies 9
authorship 19

narrative & form 21
narrative 21
framework 21
plot 25
characters 31
themes 36

style 40
direction 40
screenplay 42
mise-en-scène 45
performance 48
camera and sound 55
music 58
editing 59
a unique style 63

contexts 65
writing the third man 65
making the third man 69
the audience 74
ideologies 76
cultural 79
cinematic 83
influence 87
evaluation 90

bibliography 94
credits 96

author of this note   John Hoare is a freelance writer on literature and film. His enthusiasm for cinema as a medium began in his schooldays and has been pursued ever since. This is his first book for York Press.

background

trailer *p5*   **reading The Third Man** *p7*   **key players' biographies** *p9*
authorship *p19*

trailer

Harry Lime was just a gleam in his creator's eye early in 1947, when the novelist Graham Greene scribbled an idea for the opening of a story on the back of an envelope:

> I had paid my last farewell to Harry a week ago, when his coffin was lowered into the frozen February ground, so that it was with incredulity that I saw him pass by, without a sign of recognition, among the host of strangers in the Strand.

By the time the shooting script of *The Third Man* was completed in 1948, Harry had been transformed from an Englishman into an American and London had become Vienna; but the mystery of the 'man risen from the dead' was still the heart of the story.

The film of *The Third Man* was released in Britain in August, 1949, and was at once a huge box-office success. The film achieved comparable popular success in Europe and in the USA, and international critical admiration.

In the summer of 1999, exactly fifty years later, the film, with its print lovingly restored, was re-released in Britain and the USA. Few films achieve that triple mark of critical respect, popular affection and commercial confidence after half a century.

FROM THE PRESS IN 1949

> *The Third Man* reveals Carol Reed as probably the most brilliant craftsman of the modern cinema.
>
> Richard Winnington, *The News Chronicle*

> Carol Reed's narrative skill with camera, actors and background form a collaboration of genius and provide tensions that lift this

trailer   background

press reviews

film high out of its thriller class. Here is that orchestral handling of image, talk and music that one has looked for, so often in vain.

William Whitebait, New Statesman

The work of a craftsman so skilled that he has earned the right to be judged as an artist.

Time magazine

Just enough Orson Welles to please, not saturate ... With the aid of exceptional camerawork and carefully paced direction, the suspense of the film is well-nigh physically overpowering.

Fortnight magazine

If you insist that films should make a more personal statement, you will be dissatisfied with it and admire only its controlled perfection of technique. But as an analyst of mood and situation, Reed is practically unequalled today ...

Sight and Sound

FROM THE PRESS IN 1999

The Third Man takes the question of human badness, marries it to questions of loyalty, redemption, post-war dislocation at the heart of Europe, blesses it with an atmosphere of unprecedented comic strangeness, and in the process blows you completely away.

Andrew O'Hagan, Daily Telegraph

The Third Man captures in amber a brief, poignant moment of postwar history – the partitioned, romantic Vienna – yet remains timeless in its wit, sophistication, excitement and complex morality.

Philip French, The Observer

Of all the movies I have seen, this one most completely embodies the romance of going to the movies.

Roger Ebert, Chicago Sun-Times

To call it a classic is a statement of the obvious, but it is, and a damn fine film too.

Anwar Brett, Film Review

background — reading the third man

appeal of the film

reading the third man

The phrase 'classic' film can suggest a museum piece, but this thriller and its distinctive story and style can exert an instant magical spell today, enthralling contemporary audiences. Over the fifty years of its life, the title has passed into the language and references to the film surface regularly in contemporary films and fiction.

The Third Man is one of a kind. It joins a relatively small number of great films which endure because they have an identity which is unique – instantly recognisable. Such films defy the conventions of film genre and are impossible to label or classify in a short phrase.

Citizen Kane, *Psycho*, *The Conversation*, *Blade Runner*, *The Seventh Seal* come to mind as examples of enduring films which defy genre labelling. Their impact does not depend on style alone. In these films, the story and the way it is told are both remarkable: story and style become one. *The Third Man* is in this company.

Even after fifty years, the appeal of the film is hard to pin down – strong, almost magical, but elusive. Is it superb entertainment, great art or both? Harry Lime, the 'third man' of the title, is now part of popular mythology.

'Strangely off-beat' is how Bosley Crowther of *The New York Times* described *The Third Man* at the time of its American release. Other reviewers have used similar terms – 'quirky', 'unsettling', 'disquieting', 'occasional forays into the grotesque' – when writing about both the story and its style. Looking back in the 1960s, Pauline Kael wrote:

> *The Third Man* has a peculiar atmosphere: the sardonic, world-weary people, the sound of the zither, the baroque statues in the chic ruins, the tawdriness, are rotten but glamorous.

Few critics and fans agree exactly what this 'peculiarity' is. Part of the film's 'off-beat' nature can be found in the form of the story, part in the originality of the narrative, and part – perhaps most immediately – in its style.

reading the third man   background

trigger of the action

Consider first the form of the film, which is both thriller and romance. In what way is it odd or off-beat? As the story unfolds, *The Third Man* appears to fit comfortably into a familiar form of the detective thriller.

Holly, an American, just arrived in post-war Vienna, wants to get at the truth about how his old friend died. The police are unco-operative. As Holly starts to meet Lime's 'friends' in Vienna the mystery deepens, threats and dangers appear, there are two murders. Suddenly the mysteries are solved, his old friend is revealed to be alive, a crook in a very nasty line in crime. Holly, disillusioned, helps the police to trap his old friend and in the end shoots him dead. So far, none of this is 'peculiar' in a thriller.

Yet Holly is not a conventional amateur sleuth, who gets his man and gets the girl: Holly is bad news. An attractive, well-intentioned man, Holly has a charm not dissimilar to his friend Lime. He is also thin-skinned, impetuous, broke and boozy. Holly blunders naïvely into a world quite unfamiliar to him. We see him manipulated by friend and foe.

By the time Holly's quest has ended, he has caused one needless violent death and is indirectly responsible for two others. He has lost a boyhood hero, his best friend, and the woman he loves. Insensitive to his own blundering, he is the trigger of the action throughout the story.

He survives at the end, a poorer man in every way; but he has left disaster in his wake for almost everyone he has met in the few days of his visit. True, Holly is also responsible, by sheer accident, for clearing up the main mystery and bringing a killer to justice. But by the end of the tale, he is the last person that anyone wants to see again.

We see Holly fall in love with Anna, the beautiful mistress of his 'dead' friend. She responds to him with growing affection, but only because of his devotion to Harry's memory. Once the truth about Lime's appalling crimes starts to emerge, Holly persists in the hope that she will respond to him. But Holly cannot comprehend the nature of her loyalty to Harry, her strength, her past, her harsh experience of the world. When Holly betrays Lime to the police, Anna will have nothing more to do with him.

So, both as thriller and romance, the form of the film is not conventional. The thriller has a back-firing story with no heroes, no winners; the romance

background | biographies

deeper meanings

is an illusion. Both yield nothing but unhappiness. Yet both build and hold a knife-edge tension to the end. And, yes, the form of *The Third Man* is off-beat.

As we shall see in the next chapter, this oddness is mirrored in the plot, characterisation and themes of the film. Later, we shall look closely at the 'quirkiness' in the 'atmosphere' of the film – what the style is, what techniques build it; and how the style adds meaning to the story.

The Third Man has long since proved itself as an exciting thriller. It is difficult not to enjoy the film immediately and intensely as entertainment, as 'pure' escape. The story moves fast, the mystery appears intricate, setting and plot are novel but plausible, the crime is serious and realistic, the characters are striking. But many who have watched the film are struck also by an impression of deeper meanings, layers in the story which are elusive to the spectator on first view.

From beginning to end, and from scene to scene, there are subtexts, connotations at work. Because of their quality, *The Third Man* proves to be an enduring work of art. The layering and 'quirkiness' of its story and style add great and enduring value to the entertainment.

key players' biographies

A brilliant team of professionals made *The Third Man*. From top to bottom of the film credits, everyone behind and in front of the camera (except Hansl, the unattractive and alarming toddler) was highly skilled, striking in character and style, and very experienced. How did this exceptional gathering of talent come about?

Three key players set *The Third Man* in motion.

Just before Christmas 1947, Alexander Korda invited Graham Greene to write an original screenplay, a thriller. Carol Reed would produce and direct the film. Korda, the owner of London Films, would be the executive producer.

The three men were very different in background and character. Initially, all they had in common was a passion for films and film-making. Korda valued Reed highly as a director, but had not worked with him before 1947.

biographies   background

exceptional working relationship

At the beginning of that year Reed had come to Korda and suggested a film adaptation of a story by Graham Greene. Both Korda and Reed were admirers of Greene's fiction but had not met him. In his film reviews for *The Spectator* over the years, Greene had been strongly critical of Korda's films, principally because of their Anglo-American commercialism.

Korda and Reed invited Greene to lunch, and Greene agreed to adapt his story *The Basement Room* into the screenplay which became *The Fallen Idol*. The film proved to be a great popular and critical success both at home and in America. The making of the film forged an exceptional working relationship between the three men, and eventually a friendship which lasted well beyond the making of *The Third Man*.

Many of the millions of people who have watched *The Third Man* will be quite unaware of the names and contribution of Reed, Greene and Korda. But everyone recalls Orson Welles as Harry Lime, bestriding the film, and, for this reason, Welles must be considered a 'key player'. His impact is so powerful that it is bewildering to realise that his total appearance on screen lasts less than eleven minutes.

Two other names proved, more arguably, to be key players in very different ways: Anton Karas, the musician and David O. Selznick (American co-producer, 6,000 miles distant). Their extraordinary contributions are examined in later chapters.

The outstanding performances of Joseph Cotten, Trevor Howard and Alida Valli are memorable achievements. Robert Krasker (cinematographer), Oswald Hafenrichter (editor) and every professional before and behind the camera, played strong distinctive roles in the making of the film; and their contributions will be discussed later.

CAROL REED

In the three years following the end of the Second World War, Carol Reed made the three films which brought him huge popular success and great critical admiration in Britain, Europe and America: *Odd Man Out* (1947), *The Fallen Idol* (1948) and *The Third Man* (1949). (His films are discussed in Contexts.) Reed was forty-two years old when he directed *The Third Man*, which proved to be his masterpiece.

background biographies

meticulous preparation

Although very few people in his adult lifetime knew the secret of his parentage, Reed was the illegitimate son of Beerbohm Tree, the great Victorian actor-manager, who kept a second household in London for his mistress and her children. Reed never lived with his father. Of all Tree's children, Carol Reed resembled him most in character, looks and passion for the theatre. The secret of Reed's parentage was kept from the outside world for many years after Tree's death.

After an unhappy boarding-school life, and against the wishes of his mother, Reed joined the theatre as an actor and assistant stage manager. At the age of twenty, his abilities backstage came to the attention of Edgar Wallace, a prolific writer of thrillers in the 1920s, who made him his stage manager and personal assistant. Reed went on to manage the adaptation of a number of Wallace's stories and plays into films.

After Wallace died in 1932, Reed at the age of twenty-six moved to work with Basil Dean, the founder of Associated Talking Pictures, and worked on many of that company's cheap and undistinguished early talkies. He progressed to second-unit director, to assistant director. In 1935, he directed his first feature, *Midshipman Easy*, a moderately successful adventure film. In making these apprentice works, Reed acquired the habit of meticulous preparation and attention to detail which became a hallmark of his mature style.

The Stars Look Down, finished just as Britain was going to war in 1939, was Reed's first film to attract the serious attention of the industry and critics. During the war years Reed joined the Army's Cinematographic Service, and made several documentaries for the allied propaganda effort, two of them of feature length.

Unusually for the film industry, Reed was not a self-publicist. A modest man, obsessed with film-making, he kept both his professional and personal life out of the public eye. He gave few interviews and was reluctant to reveal much about his approach to films.

Reed's second marriage was a happy one. At home and at work, Reed was not the shy reticent figure suggested by his rare public appearance. Korda's son recalls that his house was always full of people and laughter. Reed had a strong sense of fun, sometimes uproarious humour. At work directing, he

biographies　　　　　　　background

prolific writer

was a lively incessant communicator, often boisterous, always sociable. Korda became a particularly close friend, perhaps something of a father-figure for Reed.

Of all the 'key players', the principal was Carol Reed. *The Third Man* is his film. His vision of the story, his mastery of its appearance, sound and atmosphere, his close working relationship with the actors and crew, and meticulous attention to detail, made it the unique fable that it is.

GRAHAM GREENE

The author of *The Third Man* was a prolific writer, a complex man who led a long intense life. Born in 1904, Greene lived through the two World Wars and the forty years of the Cold War. When he died in 1991, he had a literary reputation as one of the finest English novelists of the century.

Like Carol Reed, Greene had a protected middle-class childhood but was miserably unhappy at his public school in his early teens. A precocious and shy boy, he suffered intensely and secretly from bullying, not least because he was the son of the headmaster. He attempted suicide more than once.

This tormented period was to have a profound effect on his future writing. The hopes, loyalties and betrayals of schooldays, loneliness and indifferent youthful cruelty, cast a shadow in many of his novels, including *The Third Man*. He went on to study at Oxford and, shortly before his marriage in 1927, he converted to Roman Catholicism. This event, too, was to mark his life and much of his work.

Greene wrote numerous short stories, six plays, a biography, two volumes of autobiography, three travel books, screenplays, essays, reviews, literary criticism, film criticism and many journalistic pieces. He wrote twenty-three novels, of which seven were originally called by him 'Entertainments'. The novels are the achievement for which he is most remembered.

The Third Man was published as an 'Entertainment', following the success of the film. In general, the Entertainments were thrillers, stories of mystery and danger, perhaps not intended to be taken as seriously as the novels.

For many, Greene's greatest novel is *The Power and the Glory* (1940), set in Mexico, one of the handful of his novels with a strong Catholic theme, a

background biographies

pessimistic view

tragically moving story of loss and persecution. *Brighton Rock* (1938), *The Heart of the Matter* (1948), both with noticeably Catholic preoccupations and rated very highly among his novels, belong to that period before *The Third Man*. In the 1950s and 1960s, Greene's interests and fiction moved to the Far East and Latin America.

Although his later novels are no longer obviously 'Catholic', they have human themes and preoccupations similar to those in his earlier fiction. Some of his later fiction, possibly *The Comedians* or *The Honorary Consul*, may be finer novels than his better-known, earlier work.

Greene's novels perceive a damaged world in which evil is a real and pervasive force. The subjects of his work are often good men and women, in danger or moral dilemma, acting out crises in their lives, usually unhappily. There are no heroes, no happy endings. Greene once said that there were no 'black' or 'white' characters in his work, 'only black and grey'. The dramas are acted out in exotic or decaying settings: often in poor, remote countries in the grip of political violence (Vietnam, Sierra Leone, Haiti, Cuba, Mexico and others), or in a depressed England. Danger, and trials of love and loyalty, the failure of good intentions, personal treachery, of illusions sustained and lost, are frequent preoccupations of the novels.

Despite his pessimistic view of contemporary life, Greene is one of the most widely read British novelists of the twentieth century. Tension and excitement drive the stories; and flickers of hope, of love, of idealism, of innocence, light up the otherwise bleak world of his novels.

Greene was a film fan from his youngest days. He was fascinated by the cinema and film technique. From 1935 to 1940, Greene was film critic for *The Spectator*, writing more than 400 film reviews during that period. The young Dilys Powell read his reviews 'with passionate envy', John Grierson called him 'the best critic we had', Philip French thought his criticism 'the most ferocious I've ever come across'.

Greene's critical approach was forthright: 'What I object to is the idea that it is the critic's business to assist films to fulfil a social function. The critic's business should be confined to the art'; and 'The cinema has got to appeal to millions; we have got to accept its popularity as a virtue, not turn away

biographies

background

difficult man to know

from it as a vice'. He deplored the Hollywood moguls' bland assumptions of what was and was not suitable for their mass audiences: 'An excited audience is never depressed; if you excite your audience first, you can put over what you will of horror, suffering, truth'.

Greene's fascination with the cinema led him early in his career to writing for the screen. In all, he wrote screenplays for ten feature films. Four of these were versions of his own novels or stories: *Brighton Rock*, *The Fallen Idol*, *Loser Takes All*, *Our Man in Havana*. *The Third Man* was written for the screen. No fewer than twenty-two feature films were made of Greene's novels in his lifetime. None achieved the great success of *The Third Man*. With the exception of *The Confidential Agent* (1945), Greene disliked intensely the Hollywood versions of his novels.

Greene's personal life was complicated. After a few years his marriage became unhappy. Most of his life he remained separated from his wife. Greene had several long, intense affairs and many short relationships with women.

An incessant traveller, Greene spent much of his life abroad, his fascination with the effect of political struggle, with war and danger, drawing him to remote countries in every part of the world. For several years during the Second World War, Greene worked for British Intelligence as an agent for MI6, in Sierra Leone, Portugal and London.

Greene was a difficult man to know and to sum up: restless, passionate, irascible, a writer fascinated by human frailty, by frontiers. He had an appetite for adventure and compassion for the exploited individual. He combined bleak introspection with a love of literature, ideas, conversation.

In the first year of the new millennium, nine years after his death, his many novels are all in print in hardback and paperback, sell briskly and are read in almost every language in the world. Fresh biographies and memoirs of the man and his work continue to appear. It is hard to think of any other contemporary novelist who has enjoyed such a great and continuing popular success while attracting the serious attention of literary critics. *The Third Man* is his only work written solely as a film 'treatment'. It marks the half-way point in Greene's long life and achievement.

background　　　　biographies

founded London Films

ALEXANDER KORDA

Korda is a key player in the history of *The Third Man* because he was its initiator. In the volatile history of the British film industry, there have been only two movie moguls approximating in scale and power to their Hollywood models: Alexander Korda and J. Arthur Rank. Korda was active in the British industry between 1932 and his death in 1956, dominating it in the 1930s.

A professional film-maker by the age of eighteen, Korda made 141 films (ninety-nine of them in Britain) between 1916 and 1956. Of this total, he directed fifty-two, produced forty, and was executive producer of fifty-six.

Korda was born in Hungary in 1893. Before he was eighteen, he managed to get odd jobs at a film studio. By the age of twenty-three he had directed seven films in Budapest. After the First World War, he directed films in Vienna and Berlin, moving to Hollywood in the late 1920s.

Arriving in England in 1931 to work for Paramount British, Korda was thirty-eight and ambitious to build a film empire. The following year he founded London Films, which was to become synonymous with his name until his death.

From the start, Korda was determined to make British films internationally competitive. He aimed to use British stars already attractive to Hollywood, and British stories which concentrated on romance, action, humour. Many of his films were historical in setting. The year after the birth of London Films, he made *The Private Life of Henry VIII*, starring a larger-than-life Charles Laughton. It was an instant hit, an international critical and box-office success. The doors opened to American distribution.

Many of Korda's films became successful on both sides of the Atlantic, but his ambition outstripped his financial judgement. In 1938, huge debt forced the sale of London Films and Denham studios. But, as always, he bounced back.

After the war, London Films was restarted by Korda as a private company. Between 1948 and 1952, Korda was able to attract many of Britain's most talented film-makers to work with him: Carol Reed, David Lean, Powell

biographies   background

vast experience

and Pressburger, Launder and Gilliatt, and Laurence Olivier. They were drawn to Korda because, unlike Rank, he was a professional film-maker of vast experience: he gave great freedom to his directors. Korda had created the first internationally competitive film enterprise in the country.

Some years after Korda's death, Graham Greene wrote:

> There was never a man who bore less malice, and I think of him with affection – even love – as the only film producer I have ever known with whom I could spend days and nights of conversation without so much as mentioning the cinema.

An enthusiastic Anglophile, Korda was naturalised as a British citizen in 1936. Astute and ambitious, he was also a cultured and a generous man. His son David said that 'Alex ruled family and London Films both in a kind of benevolent dictatorship ...'

ORSON WELLES

Orson Welles was thirty-five years old, already a legend in cinema and theatre when he appeared in *The Third Man*. He is a key player because his Harry Lime is one of the great performances of cinema.

Born in 1915, Welles was from a very early age a child precociously gifted in the arts, an *enfant terrible* indulged by his prosperous parents. By the time he was eleven, he had travelled twice around the world. At the age of sixteen, he went to Ireland and started his professional acting career by bluffing his way into minor parts in the Dublin theatres.

Returning to America, he toured in repertory for two years and, when he was nineteen, made his New York début as Tybalt in *Romeo and Juliet*. He famously directed an all-black cast in *Macbeth* in 1936, and the following year formed the Mercury Theatre. By the age of twenty-two, Welles had achieved an international reputation as a revolutionary new talent, perhaps even a genius, of the theatre.

He had also been acting, narrating, writing and eventually producing in radio. The notorious high point of his radio career was his adaptation of H.G. Wells's *War of the Worlds*, in 1938. The novelty of presenting the story as if it were a live news broadcast caused real, unprecedented

background biographies
great cinematic performance

Lime enters the trap

biographies background

epitaph as a great actor

panic and the flight of thousands of people from their homes and from the suburbs.

When he was twenty-five, Welles signed a contract with RKO and left New York for Hollywood. He produced, directed, partly wrote and acted the lead in his first film, *Citizen Kane* (1941). This was to prove his masterpiece. *Citizen Kane* was startlingly innovative in its narrative and its cinematographic style. Welles had created a new departure for cinema, individual and original, quite distinct from contemporary Hollywood practice. Some critics believe it to be the greatest film of the century.

Citizen Kane also proved to be the highest point of Welles's career and reputation. His next film, *The Magnificent Ambersons* (1942), absorbing and full of talent, proved to be a flawed work, marred by bitter rows between Welles and the studio about finance and control. Welles and his actors of the Mercury Theatre were sacked by RKO. Welles was now out in the cold as far as the big Hollywood studios were concerned.

Some of the subsequent films in which he both directed and starred had many passages of brilliance – *Macbeth* (1948), *The Trial* (1962) and *Chimes at Midnight* (1966). *Touch of Evil* (1958) is also arguably a great film.

From the late 1940s, Welles became a professional nomad, and his ceaseless quest to finance and make his films took him frequently to Europe. The last film from the great master of illusion was *F for Fake* (1975). In the ten years between that film and his death in 1985 at the age of seventy, Welles appeared frequently in TV commercials and chat-shows, but the star had long since waned.

To the cinema-going public, Welles was an actor, a star, the Mr Rochester of *Jane Eyre* (1944). And, of course, he was Harry Lime. If the greatness of *Citizen Kane* is Orson Welles's enduring epitaph as film-maker, his performance as Harry Lime should be his epitaph as a great actor.

Unsurprisingly, Welles's private life was chaotic. His several marriages (including that with Rita Hayworth) all proved impermanent.

Welles was larger than life. His great intelligence, talent, wit, charm and energy invested a ruthless egotism with a magnetism that seemed to

background

authorship

harmonious partnership

sweep all, or almost all, before it. He was consistent in his conviction that he was a genius, and in his need to fulfil that genius in theatre and cinema.

authorship

> I think it is the director's job – as in the old theatre – to convey faithfully what the author had in mind. Unless you have worked with the author in the first place you cannot convey to the actors what he had in mind nor can you convey to the editor at the end the original idea.
>
> Reed, interviewed by Robert Ginna in Horizon

Sooner or later, the question is raised: 'whose film was it?' In the case of *The Third Man*, the answer is quite clear: there are two authors. It is Greene's story but Carol Reed's film. Reed is not the author, or an auteur; but we shall see that the script owed much to his creativity.

There have been successive waves of interpretations of the meaning of auteur and auteur theory since their first use in French film criticism in the 1920s. Central to most definitions is the idea of the director writing (or originating) and controlling the story and film-making throughout. *Citizen Kane* is an auteur film; and *The Third Man* is not. But the story of the authorship of *The Third Man* may be more intriguing than any debate about the value of auteurs. What happened in practice is unusual in the world of film-making.

THE NOVELIST AND THE DIRECTOR

The first unusual feature in the origin of *The Third Man* is that a famous novelist (Greene) was contracted to write an original 'film play' – any story based on his one-paragraph idea – so long as it was set in Vienna. Almost as unusual is the way that Greene and Reed later worked together on the screenplay, through successive drafts. It was a close, harmonious partnership.

This kind of intense collaboration between writer and director is, perhaps, rare. (Greene and Reed had worked in a similar fashion a year earlier on the

authorship — background

draft screenplay

screenplay for *The Fallen Idol*.) They had taken a suite of rooms in a Brighton hotel with interconnecting rooms. Greene wrote and re-wrote, and they discussed every page, both men suggesting and discussing changes to plot, action, dialogue and script. The screenplay was completed in ten days by this method.

In June 1948, Greene travelled to Vienna with Reed to transform his 'film treatment' (novel) of *The Third Man* into a draft screenplay. They worked together in the same way as they had on *The Fallen Idol* (see Contexts: Writing *The Third Man*).

In the Preface to *The Fallen Idol*, Greene wrote the following:

> Of one thing about both these films [*The Fallen Idol* and *The Third Man*] I have complete certainty, that their success is due to Carol Reed, the only director I know with that particular warmth of human sympathy, the extraordinary feeling for the right face for the right part, the exactitude of cutting, and not least important the power of sympathising with an author's worries and an ability to guide him.

narrative & form

narrative *p21*   **framework** *p21*   **plot** *p25*
characters *p31*   **themes** *p36*

narrative

The main function of a feature film is to tell a story. At its simplest, a film's narrative is the story that it tells. In this sense of the word, the narrative is made up of the story-line, dialogue, action, characters and themes.

But there is a definition of film narrative which is richer than this. This view takes the narrative to be the whole film text – the combination of everything that the viewer sees and hears in the film. We shall look at this richer definition of film text as it applies to *The Third Man* at the beginning of the next chapter, because it is inseparable from the effect of the style on the narrative. In this chapter we concentrate on the story and its dimensions: its overall structure, framework and the plot, characters, and themes that work within it.

STRUCTURE

The structure of the narrative has several dimensions: plot, character, theme; and an overall framework. In the best films, the unity of this structure ensures the smooth flow of the narrative: the audience is captured by the momentum of the whole. But the dimensions can be looked at separately with advantage.

In *The Third Man*, each dimension of the narrative structure (framework, plot, characters and theme) has its own intricacy. Layers of meaning contribute to the 'off-beat' nature of the whole.

framework

The framework of the story is essentially the envelope of time, place and point of view which bounds (contains) the action. The framework within which the story of *The Third Man* unfolds is very tight and unified as to time and place. The point of view from which the audience 'reads' the film

framework narrative & form

reversals and revelations

is less clear-cut. We shall see that there is a marked change, the point of view shifting steadily as the story unfolds.

TIME

The year is 1948, three years after the end of the Second World War. The season, appropriate to the story, is winter. It is the dead end of the year, late November, early December. Although snow has not yet arrived in Vienna, we see that it is imminent. The days are cold and dull, the nights colder, dark and damp. About half the film consists of night scenes. We are left with the impression that the whole story is enacted in a cold night-time, or wintry twilight.

The action of *The Third Man* takes place in the seven days between Harry's first and final funerals: just one week between Holly's arrival and departure. So many reversals and revelations occur in the plot, and the cutting between scenes is so sharp, that to the audience the action appears to be continuous, 'real' time.

PLACE

The entire action takes place in Vienna, virtually all within the historic inner city. Vienna is an active player in the story, not just an 'interesting' cinematic location. Although the main players of the story are foreigners in the city, we see at every moment how each of these expatriates has to cope with the challenges thrown in his or her path by the city, whether by its bleakness, by some of its demoralised or criminal citizens, or by its imposed and foreign government.

At the time of the story and the filming of *The Third Man*, the aftermath of war was strikingly visible in Vienna. For many of its people, the war had ended savagely. Poverty, hunger and crime, particularly black-market traffic, were still widespread. We see Austria under military occupation. The victorious allies, Soviet Russia, Britain, USA and France, each govern one zone of the capital. The Inner City is a separate zone, governed collectively by all four powers, policed by an international military patrol. We see this patrol, in jeeps and in action, several times in the film. The narrator comments ironically:

narrative & form # framework

post-war wreckage

> One member of each of the four powers. What a hope they had, all strangers to the place and none of them could speak the same language, except for a sort of smattering of German ... Good fellows on the whole ...

The occupying powers take turn, one month at a time, to command this international force. During the action of the story, Major Calloway is in charge.

> I never knew the old Vienna before the war, with its Strauss music, its glamour and easy charm – Constantinople suited me better. I really got to know it in the classic period of the Black Market ...

says the anonymous narrator in the opening words of the film.

'Old' Vienna plays no active part in the story. But it is strongly present, like a ghost, offering mute comment on the post-war wreckage. The monuments of Vienna's great centuries provide a counterpoint to the present ruins and squalor of the city. We see reminders of that grandeur in the baroque statuary, the imperial architecture, the elaborate domestic interiors, the ruined pleasure gardens, the cemetery, the ambitious sewers, the play at the Josefstadt Theatre. Always in our ears is a sort of echo of that past, a voice of Vienna, in the haunting zither music of Anton Karas.

POINT-OF-VIEW

From what point of view does the narrative unfold its story in *The Third Man*? There are really two points of view in the film text, one less obvious than the other:

Holly's story: We see Holly on the screen for all but six minutes of the film. For the first hour, the point of view is subjective, almost 'first person'. We are encouraged to see the action as if we were in Holly's shoes. We are with him as he arrives in Vienna so optimistically and bounds up the staircase

framework

narrative & form

distancing the viewer

to Lime's flat. We identify with him and his quest for the truth as he encounters the successive mysteries surrounding Harry's death. We meet Calloway, Kurz, Winkel, Anna, through Holly's eyes. It is almost as if Holly were the 'I' of the story.

But the point of view begins to shift, becomes more objective. With Holly's crucial discovery that Lime is alive, the 'first person' view disappears altogether. As the story moves faster to its violent and melancholy climax, the viewer is increasingly distanced from him. It is no longer Holly's story. We are looking at it through the sardonic eyes of a detached observer. Unseen and unheard, he is the teller of the story. We have heard him at the very start of *The Third Man*.

The narrator's story: As the credits dissolve, the film opens with a rapid montage of scenes of war-damaged Vienna. The voice of an unseen narrator (played by Carol Reed) introduces us to the realities of the city under allied occupation. His voice is English, educated, casual. He talks quickly, with the hint of a much-travelled man, well-acquainted with crime and the seamy side of cosmopolitan cities. We see the 'Shot of a body floating in an icy river':

```
Of course, a situation like that does tend to happen
to amateurs - but you know they can't stay the
course like a professional.
```

The technique has the function of distancing the viewer from the protagonists before we even see them. The device has been used frequently in fiction, but is not common in film. In this case, it is almost a warning to the viewer not to identify too closely with Holly:

```
Oh wait, I was going to tell you - I was going to
tell you about Holly Martins from America - he came
all the way here to visit a friend of his. The name
was Lime, Harry Lime. Now Martins was broke and Lime
had offered him - I don't know - some sort of job.
Anyway, there he was, poor chap, happy as a lark
and without a cent.
```

narrative & form

plot

linear succession of discoveries

It is the only time we hear the narrator in the film. But in the intense last thirty minutes of the film we are no longer in Holly's shoes. We are deeply involved in the tangle of lives of the three main characters, but not from Holly's point of view. These almost tragic sequences are seen through the detached, ironic eyes of the invisible narrator.

plot

The 'plot' is the story-line: the ordering of the sequence of events and actions that make up the narrative.

The Third Man is a thriller: the events and surprises must have sufficient reality and plausibility for the audience to accept them and want more. The plot of *The Third Man* passes this test with ease. Many surprises, dangers and reverses are packed at a smart pace into the 104 minutes of the film.

The plot is well crafted both as a thriller and as romance. The characters are distinctive but convincing. Their motivation is strong and the story-line flows naturally.

The crime and tensions of the plot are plausible and authentic: crime *was* rife in Vienna at the time, there *was* a lethal penicillin racket, the sewers *were* used illegally for travel between occupied zones, the Russians *did* forcibly repatriate East European nationals by any means available, life *was* very hard for most of the population. The narrative moves rapidly, a series of connecting mysteries, surprises and partial revelations which builds suspense expertly. The ending does not disappoint.

PLOT STRUCTURE

The events of the plot of *The Third Man* are intricate, but the shape of the plot is both simple and elegant. It uses a narrative sequence common to most fiction and 'classic Hollywood cinema', a sequence of order-disorder-order restored.

The opening establishes a momentary equilibrium (introducing Vienna and Holly). The first major shock ('disorder') of the story comes less than two minutes into the film: Lime has died and his funeral is now. This shock sets off a linear succession of discoveries and events, ending only with Lime's 'second' death, in a kind of exhausted equilibrium.

plot

narrative & form

> hook for the audience

The elegance of the plot is that the entire action occurs between two major events which appear to be identical – the two funerals of Harry Lime. These parallel events give the story a symmetry which is both witty and eerie.

MAIN PLOT

Crucial discoveries

Between the time that he arrives in Vienna and his departure, Holly makes twelve crucial discoveries about Harry. Each is a shock, prompting Holly into a new course of action. (The sequence of these discoveries is shown in Discoveries opposite, a guide to the structure of the plot and a reminder of its pace.)

Each discovery is, of course, also a hook for the audience, a twist in the plot which sparks off new speculation about the direction the story is taking.

Two-thirds of the story pass before the most dramatic shock of the film, the key revelation. This is Holly's sudden glimpse of Lime, very much alive and fit, in the doorway opposite Anna's flat. This moment is the hinge of the plot. The two parts of the plot, before and after this moment, have different motors driving the action. The first part is *mystery*, the second is *pursuit* and *painful choices*.

Part One – How did Lime die?

The mystery is the first and longer part of the plot. Holly assumes the role of amateur investigator (or perhaps of one of his characters, *The Lone Rider of Santa Fe*) and drives the story along. The mystery changes from 'Was it an accident?' to 'Who murdered him and why?' to 'Who was the third man with Kurz and Popescu?'. The key revelation – 'I've just seen a dead man walking' – solves these mysteries in a second, but immediately creates a crisis in the action and different, tougher problems for the characters.

Part Two – The hunt for Lime

From the moment we know that Harry Lime lives, the plot becomes driven by Lime, Calloway and Anna. *The Third Man* is still the story of Holly: the fateful decision ('All right, Callaghan, you win ... I'll be your dumb decoy duck') is his alone. But now we see Holly caught between three powerful individuals, each with a will stronger than his.

narrative & form

plot

key events

Discoveries
Guide to the key events in the plot of *The Third Man*

- Seven of these discoveries mark a **turning point** in the story and are marked in **bold**.
- The true **hinge** of the plot is Discovery No. 8.
- The numbered scenes refer to the Faber and Faber edition of the **screenplay**.

Main plot (Holly)

Scene	No.	Event		Discovery
Lime's flat	9	Holly meets porter: 'he was killed at once.'	1	Lime is dead, in road accident
Bar	14	Holly drinks with Calloway after funeral.	2	Lime was a black market racketeer
Outside Lime's flat	18	Kurz: 'Popescu and I carried him'	3	Two of Lime's friends were the only witnesses to the accident
Lime's flat	28	Porter tells Holly –	4	**'There was a third man'**
Outside Lime's flat	60	Holly, Anna, Hansl, crowd	5	**Porter has been murdered**
Cultural Centre	70	Holly on the run, suspected of Porter's murder	6	Holly now a police suspect, and Lime's friends want him dead
Calloway's office	81	Calloway: 'These were murders'	7	Graphic evidence that Lime ran lethal penicillin racket. Holly convinced
Outside Anna's flat	95	Holly spots Lime, gives futile chase	8	**Lime is alive**
Kiosk, square	96	Calloway: 'I've been a fool.'	9	Lime uses Vienna's sewers for undetected travel between zones
Great Wheel	114	Holly to Lime: 'You informed on her.'	10	**Lime has betrayed Anna to the Russians**
Great Wheel	116	Lime to Holly: 'Free of income tax, old man.'	11	Lime will kill Holly unless he leaves Vienna or works for Lime
Children's hospital	124, 125	Calloway:- 'awful pity'. Holly:- 'I'll be your dumb decoy duck'.	12	**Appalling human effects of Lime's racket**

Subplot (Anna)

Scene	No.	Event		Discovery
Calloway's office	106	Anna: 'It is true, then?'	1	Lime is alive
Railway station	120	Anna: 'Poor Harry'	2	Holly has decided to help the police trap Lime

THE THIRD MAN

plot

breathtaking sequence

narrative & form

Anna and Holly.
The long goodbye

THE THIRD MAN

narrative & form plot

romantic subplot

Three breathtaking sequences illustrate this shift in the plot: the confrontation between Holly and Lime in the Great Wheel, the manhunt in the sewers; and the final shot in the cemetery. Lime dominates the first, Lime and Calloway the second, Anna the third.

In the Wheel, Holly is appalled by Lime's cold-blooded ruthlessness, but not enough to help Calloway in the hunt for Lime. Only the revelation that Lime has betrayed Anna to the Russians leads Holly to agree to help trap Lime, in exchange for Anna's safety. A miserable Holly withdraws from this pact when Anna refuses the safe passage. Holly is only persuaded again to lure Lime into an ambush when Calloway batters his conscience, tricking him into a visit to the children's ward where a number of Lime's victims are maimed or dying.

At the end of the chase in the sewers, Holly comes upon the badly wounded Lime, mutely wanting death in preference to prison. Lime gives the faintest of nods to his old friend. Holly shoots and kills him.

The end

After Lime's death and second funeral, Holly waits for Anna in the long avenue of the cemetery. He leans on a handcart, smoking. In the distance, Anna walks steadily towards him (and us). She is now very close and 'she pays no attention, walking right past him and on into the distance'.

Holly is now quite alone, due to leave Vienna much as he arrived, 'without a cent', but no longer 'happy as a lark'.

SUBPLOT

The romantic subplot, Anna's story, develops alongside the main plot and eventually fuses with it. Holly first sees Anna at Lime's funeral, silent and grieving. Holly seeks her out, and rapidly falls in love with her. At first unresponsive, she thaws slowly, but she remains Harry's girl. Anna is neither surprised by nor interested in the possibility that Harry was a dangerous black marketeer: 'A man doesn't alter because you've found out more'. Only when she learns that Harry is, in fact, alive does she seem to become alive again herself.

plot — narrative & form

farcical interlude

The Russian threat

But Anna has a problem, apparently unconnected with Harry's death. She is an illegal immigrant from Czechoslovakia with a forged passport. The Russians in Vienna somehow discover this and want to extradite her to Czechoslovakia. Calloway offers that if she co-operates in the investigation into Lime, he will protect her from arrest by the Russians. Anna will not help Calloway.

The subplot becomes one with the main plot when Holly realises that it is Lime who has betrayed Anna to the Russians. Holly makes a deal with Calloway: Holly will co-operate to find Lime, if Calloway will protect Anna from deportation.

Anna is on her way to freedom when she suddenly realises what Holly has done: she is to be the price of Lime's entrapment:

```
'I don't want to see him, hear him. But he's in me
– that's a fact. I wouldn't do a thing to harm him.'
```

She tears up her ticket to safety and walks away.

```
(CALLOWAY sourly: 'A girl of spirit')
```

She will have nothing more to do with Holly. Later, when she finds Holly waiting in the café to trap Lime, the 'dumb decoy duck', Anna enables Lime to escape.

INTERLUDE

This unconventional plot becomes more off-beat with a short farcical interlude. This is the episode at the Cultural Centre, in which Holly finds himself obliged to discuss 'the future of the novel' with an audience of Viennese literary buffs.

Early in his stay in Vienna, Holly the pulp writer has been mistaken for a famous novelist of a more serious kind. Crabbin, a British Council representative desperate for a speaker, offers to pay his hotel bill if Holly will lecture at a literary evening in a few days' time.

Holly (and the audience) promptly forgets about this obligation. Much later Holly, on the run from Popescu, jumps into a taxi outside the hotel. After a

narrative & form characters

welcome contrast

frightening ride, he finds that the grim, silent driver has brought him to the Cultural Centre and an impatient audience.

The 'discussion' of course is a comic fiasco. We are shown only a few shots of it – the earnest questions near the end, a bewildered audience and even more bewildered Holly, the dismay of Crabbin:

```
AUSTRIAN MAN: James Joyce – now where would you put
him – in what category?
HOLLY: Would you mind repeating the question?
```

This interlude is cunningly placed. The comedy takes us by surprise and is funny, the contrast welcome after non-stop suspense. But we are not kept long from the tensions of the plot. Popescu has also arrived, and from the audience poses veiled, threatening questions. As the meeting breaks up in disarray, Holly makes his escape and finds his way to Calloway.

characters

The characters of *The Third Man* are vivid, as in a short story. They come fully formed from the moment we see each of them. In the course of the seven days of the story, the characters do not develop, though our perception of them does. While Holly's understanding changes slowly from illusion to disillusion, he does not change, probably *cannot* change.

Holly, Lime, Anna and Calloway create the drama from their intense interaction with each other, each with a view of the world quite different from that of the others.

HOLLY

When we first see Holly, he seems to personify American get-up-and-go, the 'can-do' attitude. He bounds up the stairs to Lime's flat with energy and confidence, no hint that he is broke and glad of 'some kind of job'. In less than two minutes, the serenity has disappeared but the 'can-do' persists disastrously, almost to the end of his unhappy visit to Vienna.

We learn that Holly writes pulp fiction, paperback Westerns. His books have sold well in the past, but now barely provide him with a living. His values

characters

Holly is foolish

in real life seem to reflect those of his Westerns, worthy but simplistic: the right of the homesteader to stand up to the cattle bosses, loyalty to your buddy, the truth-seeker frustrated by the complacent sheriff.

Arriving in a distant country, Holly is ignorant of the language and uninterested in the strangeness of the battered city. His quest throughout the story is that of an innocent abroad.

Lads together

Anna says of Lime, 'He never grew up. The world grew up around him'. She comes to believe the same about Holly Martins. Anna calls Holly 'Harry' on two separate occasions. In some ways, Holly is an unwitting reflection of Lime. Holly's loyalty and devotion to Lime derive from escapades of their schooldays and young manhood. His old hero-worship motivates the action. He shares a kind of immaturity with Lime; but Lime is the more perceptive of the two men:

```
LIME: We aren't heroes, Holly, you and I. The world
doesn't make heroes outside your books.
```

and a little later:

```
HOLLY: You've never grown up, Harry.
LIME: Well, we shall be old for a very long time.
```

Impulsiveness

Holly has the virtue of courage: he is prepared to take on enemies who threaten his values. He also drinks a lot and, as Calloway notes in the novel, is likely to 'turn unpleasant after the fourth glass'. His courage is of the impulsive and unrewarding kind.

He is also impulsive in love: he falls for Anna minutes after meeting her. As she walks out of his life at the close of the story, we can only speculate how he feels, what he might do.

Loser

Worse than innocent, Holly is foolish. His ignorance and moral tunnel-vision lead him into blunders which have disastrous consequences for

narrative & form   characters

brooding presence

other people. In their different ways, Calloway, Lime, Anna and Lime's friends all consider Holly a foolish nuisance. They deal with him only because each of them needs something from him.

```
HOLLY: A parrot bit me.
CALLOWAY: Oh, stop behaving like a fool, Martins.
```

By the end Holly has lost everything. The woman he has fallen in love with has only contempt for him. Everything that he had admired about his buddy Lime – the daring, the risky escapades – all are now revealed as sham. Holly had been the patsy, the fall guy, 'Safe for you: not safe for me'.

But Holly is a loser who does not know he is a loser. Even at the end of the story, amid the human wreckage, rejected by everyone, has Holly given up? Is he a man redeemed, changed by this experience? Or will he fall for a new pretty face, a new job offer, on the long journey home?

LIME

For sixty-two minutes of the story we do not see Harry Lime, but his presence broods over every scene. Although Holly is rarely out of camera shot, Lime is rarely absent from the dialogue. From the outset he is a figure of power and mystery.

A disturbing outline of Lime – part god, part devil – emerges from the contradictory perceptions of the other characters: Anna's passionate love, Holly's devotion ('Best friend I ever had'); Calloway's contempt: 'about the worst racketeer that ever made a dirty living in this city'.

Even with this build-up, we are unprepared for his resurrection and the magnitude of his personality.

Lime has only one scene (exactly five minutes) in which we see and hear the man clearly. The memorable fairground ride in the Great Wheel is the first meeting between Holly and Lime for nine years. What does Lime reveal about himself in this short time? We see that he is a complex man, with at least the following characteristics:

- *Quick-witted* – Lime thinks and acts fast;
- *Charming* – he has wit and cheek of an exceptional kind, can manipulate

characters

great speech

even old friends with the total assurance of the born con-man ('Think it over, old man ...');

■ *Amoral* – he reveals ruthless self-interest, indifference to others, an amoral disregard of the consequences of his crimes ('Victims? Don't be melodramatic');

■ *Lethal* – we see that he is an experienced killer, immediately ready to get rid of Holly or anyone else threatening his schemes or survival.

These come together in Lime's great speech at the topmost point of the Wheel. This is the 'heart of darkness' of *The Third Man*. Impatient with Holly's use of the word 'victims', he points to the passers-by far below:

```
'Would you really feel any pity if any one of those
dots stopped moving forever? If I said you can have
twenty thousand pounds for every dot that stops,
would you really, old man, tell me to keep my money
- or would you calculate how many dots you could
afford to spare? Free of income tax, old man, free
of income tax. (He gives his boyish, conspiratorial
smile.) It's the only way to save nowadays.'
```

As the camera peers down at what are indeed dots far below, Lime is like Mephistopheles, the devil's lieutenant on earth. Taking Holly to a high place, he tempts him by offering the riches of the world at insignificant cost.

ANNA

Anna at first seems to be a passive, recurring victim of the story. When we meet her, she is alone, far from a home she cannot return to: a victim of the war or of the cold war. She is grieving for Harry, her one source of happiness. Later, Anna is betrayed cynically by Lime, hounded by the Russians, and used as a bargaining counter by Calloway in his hunt for Lime. It is only because of their shared love for Harry that Anna listens to Holly. She never takes seriously his 'falling in love' with her.

Yet it is Anna who emerges from the action as the strongest character, the one person who does not swerve in love and loyalty, the one with enough

narrative & form — characters

setting the trap

courage to hold to her principles and act upon them. When she discovers near the end that Holly has agreed to entrap Lime, Anna is yet again a victim. But Anna, still courageous, is no longer passive. She

- tears up her ticket and papers to freedom;
- alerts Harry to the trap, throwing herself into the line of fire so that he can escape;
- cuts Holly dead, discards him and her safety completely.

CALLOWAY

Major Calloway is a cool customer: a shrewd and skilful policeman and soldier. He proves to be Lime's nemesis. Calloway does not suffer fools (Holly) gladly:

```
CALLOWAY: He's only a scribbler with too much drink
in him.
```

We know little about Calloway the man: part of his job is to conceal his emotions. But we do have brief glimpses of a humanity (in the hospital and with Anna) behind the single-minded pursuit of Lime. Calloway is laconic, with a dry wit ('This isn't Santa Fe, I'm not a sheriff, and you aren't a cowboy ...'). A man of his word, Calloway will keep his part of a bargain. Not an unkind man, he appears to Holly and Anna to be unsympathetic, sometimes hateful.

Above all, Calloway is a professional. Incorruptible and smart, he is not infallible. Tricked by Lime's 'burial' like everyone else ('I've been a fool. We should have dug deeper than a grave'), he makes up for his mistake by his skill in setting the trap for Lime.

Calloway considers Holly a foolish hindrance, except for his knowledge of Lime, which might have a use. Calloway has no hesitation in exploiting both Holly and Anna. The major is quick to use his authority to rescue Anna from deportation, in return for Holly's help in trapping Lime. But his good will to Anna is purely professional and cuts out automatically when Holly reneges on the deal. As a last and successful effort to win Holly's co-operation, he tricks him into viewing the dying victims of Lime's racket.

characters   narrative & form

brilliant cameos

THE VIENNESE

Each of these local citizens has a highly individual role in drawing us into the layers of mystery.

Lime's three Viennese 'friends' are brilliantly written cameos: seedy, off-beat denizens of Greeneland. These crooks, the 'baron', the doctor and 'businessman' are cunning and sophisticated survivors of war and crime. Comically banal but dangerous, this sinister trio is united only by greed.

By contrast, two 'good' Viennese – Lime's porter and Anna's landlady – offer us a glimpse of ordinary citizens trying to survive in the post-war city. Both are inured and resigned to alien military occupation, both watchful, angry: one fearful, the other eccentric, perpetually indignant.

themes

Apart from the immediate meaning of *The Third Man* as a thriller and romance, what is it *about*? What are the underlying human issues of the story, the preoccupations of its authors?

As in most memorable films and novels, there are subtexts, unstated messages, under the surface of the film text. Subtexts are always open to debate. What follows is a personal interpretation.

The Third Man has several related themes or subtexts. The messages are delivered with wit, but none of them is optimistic.

When a French critic in the 1940s pronounced the novelist's name as 'Grim Grin', he unwittingly made an apt commentary on Greene's pessimistic irony.

DEADLY INNOCENCE

The Third Man is sparked and fuelled throughout by Holly's blundering quest to do the right thing. The story illustrates the destructive power of innocence – particularly of well-meaning interference. The naïve person, intent on righting a wrong, can damage more than he or she mends.

As a direct result of Holly's actions in the story, three men (the Porter, Paine and Lime) die violently, two of them undeservedly:

narrative & form   themes

destructive innocence

■ Although Holly suspects the smooth Popescu of murdering Harry, he tells him that the porter was a witness to the 'accident'. The porter is murdered shortly after.

■ In the sewers, Holly ignores Calloway's order to stay close, impetuously rushes out to follow Lime, and Paine is killed trying to get Holly to safety.

■ Holly, with a wink of acquiescence from Lime, shoots dead his badly wounded friend to save him from the prospect of a life sentence or worse. But, of course, it is Holly who has lured his friend into this impasse.

Easy to overlook, the theme of Holly's destructive innocence is subtly mirrored by those archetypal innocents, animals and a small child:

■ The neighbours' small boy Hansl identifies Holly as the foreigner who was with the porter shortly before his murder. Hansl sets off the chase of Holly as murder suspect – 'Papa, Papa ...'

■ Anna's kitten – 'He only liked Harry' – discovers the invisible Lime in a dark doorway, rubs on his shoe and mews loudly in pleasure, attracting Holly's attention: 'What kind of a spy do you think you are, satchelfoot?'. This, in turn, causes a neighbour to switch on the light which reveals Lime's face.

■ Kurz's dog betrays the presence of his master (and Winkel's friendship with Kurz) when it wanders into Holly's questioning of Dr Winkel – 'That your dog?' 'Yes' –

■ A parrot squawks in the room as Holly is trying to escape Popescu and his thugs, betraying his presence. When Holly tries to hush it, the parrot bites his hand.

These brief incidents are at the same time funny and pessimistic. The unwitting power of these small innocents to betray their 'masters', slily reinforces the theme.

BETRAYAL

Betrayal is a recurring act in *The Third Man* and a persistent theme in most of Greene's fiction.

themes   narrative & form

trail of damage

Lime betrays Anna to the Russians, informing them of her origin and false passport, in return for Russian protection from Calloway. Lime will also betray his friendship with Holly (or with anyone) and kill him without hesitation if necessary.

Holly himself is prepared to betray Lime, as a trade-off for Anna's safety. But this is not mainly because of his disgust with Lime's work: he hopes to become Anna's lover. Without the prize of Anna's company, Holly abandons the deal. Eventually he is shamed by Calloway into betrayal by the sight of the suffering in the children's ward, and he lures his best friend into a police trap.

Anna alone is constant. Rightly or wrongly, she remains committed to her lover:

```
'I don't want him any more. I don't want to see
him, hear him. But he's in me - that's a fact. I
wouldn't do a thing to harm him.'
```

When Anna realises that Lime's capture is to be the price for her freedom, she rejects her safety, and Holly with it.

Betrayal leads to loss. In *The Third Man*, everyone loses. Although a sort of justice is achieved in the end and an evil man is brought down, Holly leaves a trail of damage and loss.

Lime has lost his criminal empire and his life. Anna has lost her lover, her suitor, her safe refuge. Kurz, Winkel and Popescu lose their freedom, in jail. Calloway, in one way a winner, has lost Paine, his highly valued sergeant: a huge loss for a small gain.

Holly has lost his 'best friend', his new love, his job prospects; and the respect of all around him. He has also lost a hero and the illusions of his youth.

FALLEN WORLD

Post-war Vienna of *The Third Man* can be seen as a metaphor for the world in the twentieth century. The wreckage and darkness of Vienna are a striking exemplar of a Europe which has been shattered, physically and morally.

narrative & form — themes

malign force

The characters move in a fallen world, a world in which old certainties and values have collapsed. This is the morally bankrupt world which is home to Lime.

Lime and his cronies are driven by greed and opportunism. The tools for survival in this world are ruthlessness, sharp-wittedness and insensitivity to human damage.

EVIL

There is a subtext of evil, not just mere badness, in *The Third Man*. In his novels, Greene returned again and again to the reality of evil as a malign force in the world; and we can feel its presence in this story. The whisper of hidden, deep corruption starts with the conversations with Kurz, Winkel and Popescu; and emerges dramatically in the person of Lime.

In the Great Wheel, Lime's nihilism, his amused justification of the deadly penicillin racket and of murder, his indifference to Anna's fate, reveal something which surpasses criminality. The ruthlessness is all the more frightening for the relaxed good humour of its delivery, the twinkle in the eye.

Lime is perhaps a twentieth-century equivalent of the devil's ambassador. Like Mephistopheles, Lime takes Holly to a high place to survey the world below, threatening and tempting him at the same time:

> 'I'd like to cut you in, you know. We always did things together, Holly. I've no one left in Vienna I can really trust.'

Beyond love or morality, the devil's salesman offers Holly a new lease of life, promising riches:

> 'Free of income tax, old man, free of income tax.'

style

direction *p40* **screenplay** *p42* **mise-en-scène** *p45* **performance** *p48*
camera and sound *p55* **music** *p58* **editing** *p59* **a unique style** *p63*

The director creates the style of the film. But what is style?

The veteran director Sidney Lumet offers a straightforward definition. Style, he says, is simply 'the way you tell a particular story'. Lumet goes on to say that he has to make two critical decisions at the outset of making a film. The first decision is 'What's this story about?' (the themes). The second decision is 'Now that I know **what** it's about, **how** shall I tell it?'. How best can the techniques of filming be used to express the content of the story?

FILM TEXT

Reading the screenplay may give a first impression of the style of a film; but only by *reading the film text*, by viewing the film, can we truly experience its style. Story and film style should unite in the film text.

This chapter considers the style of *The Third Man* and the techniques that contribute to it under seven main headings:

- Direction
- Screenplay
- Mise-en-scène
- Performance
- Music
- Camera and sound
- Editing

and concludes with a pointer to the unique style of the film.

direction

Carol Reed's vision of the story and his work with the writer, performers and crew created the final text and style of *The Third Man*.

style direction

illuminating the themes

IMAGERY

A major recurring contribution to the overall style of the film is Reed's creation of a visual *imagery*. The imagery uses combinations of performance, light, camera and sound to illuminate powerfully the themes of the story, as well as to create the tension and excitement of the thriller.

The imagery of anxiety

■ Mazes and obstacles seem to hinder Holly throughout: narrow streets, barred windows, tunnels, winding stairs, the bad-luck ladder at the start, military bureaucracy.

■ The recurring use of height suggests Holly's vulnerability in alien surroundings – staircases and buildings rise steeply from him, the Great Wheel endangers him.

■ Height again serves a different purpose for Lime, suggesting both his threat and almost supernatural power. We only see Lime for a few seconds on the ground: he is either high above the earth (Wheel, rubble mountain) or in the underworld (sewers).

■ Ordinary, everyday things threaten: the small child, the parrot, the taxi driver.

■ The use of German dialogue, incomprehensible to Holly, whenever any of the Viennese talk or shout to anyone except him. *Alienation* is part of the style.

The light and the dark

The contrast of light and dark continually heightens the action and atmosphere of the film.

■ The darkness and shadows (of the streets, the sewers, some interiors) emphasise the darkness of the themes and the tensions in the characters. When light suddenly illuminates a face (Lime, Calloway, sentry, child) the effect is startling rather than reassuring.

■ The light brings little relief by contrast. Daylight scenes (the cemetery, Lime's flat) and bright interior scenes (the night club, police station) have a flat, grey, comfortless quality.

direction — style

meticulous attention

REED'S STYLE

The individual style of each of Reed's films was tailored to the story he chose, and was not repeated: his signature is engraved beneath the surface. The director he admired most was William Wyler. Reed once commented, 'The brilliance of Wyler's technique lies in its concealment'.

Reed paid meticulous attention to preparation, to every element of story and style, to every detail of filming, and to every second of the final cut. This attention to detail might be said to be his signature, the hallmark of a great craftsman. But it is, of course, an invisible signature that is only appreciated consciously after several viewings.

The extraordinary atmosphere of *The Third Man* is Reed's creation. It comes from his inner reading of the story and how it should be presented. We can recognise many of the elements that contribute to that vision, but find it difficult to define the whole.

screenplay

> The really essential thing is a good script. With that, the rest is easy.
>
> *Carol Reed, interviewed by Dilys Powell*

The style of Greene's story and screenplay is both the foundation and a strong component of the style of the film. Some pointers to that style, which are characteristic of Greene's fiction, are outlined below.

GREENELAND

The Vienna of *The Third Man* is recognisable as part of 'Greeneland', a setting of much of Greene's work. Greeneland is found wherever his characters struggle with their lives at home or abroad. Sometimes seedy, Greeneland is an unreliable everyday world; there are threats, passions, disappointed hopes and betrayals.

Pessimistic about the human condition, Greene used simple language and taut dialogue to express strikingly a complex view of life. A characteristic

style

screenplay

naming characters

example of Greene's style from the novel *The Ministry of Fear* – 'Pity is the worst passion of all: we don't outlive it like sex'.

The style of Greeneland glimmers through the screenplay and dialogue of *The Third Man*:

```
LIME: In these days, old man, nobody thinks in
terms of human beings. Governments don't, so why
should we? They talk of the people and the
proletariat, and I talk of the mugs. It's the same
thing.

That shade of melancholy crosses LIME's face.

HOLLY: You used to believe in God.

LIME: Oh, I still believe, old man. In God and
Mercy and all that. The dead are happier dead. They
don't miss much here, poor devils.
```

As he speaks the last words with a touch of genuine pity, the car reaches the platform ...

```
LIME: What do you believe in?
```

Lime's question remains unanswered.

Names

The naming of his characters was important to Greene, part of his style. The names of Calloway, Kurz, Crabbin, like many in his novels, carry associations of hardness, coldness, decay or seediness.

Holly was 'Rollo' in the novel. Greene had conceived of Rollo as an appropriately foolish name for his character. Joseph Cotten was unhappy with the name, and Greene suggested 'Holly' as a worthy substitute.

As for Harry Lime, Greene later revealed: 'I wanted for my "villain" a name natural and yet disagreeable, and to me "Lime" represented the quick-lime in which murderers were said to be buried'.

screenplay style

ironic visual touches

DIALOGUE

With the exception of Lime's persuasive speeches in the Wheel, the dialogue consists mainly of short exchanges. The style is often biting:

```
HOLLY: You can't order me around, Callaghan. I'm
going to get to the bottom of this.
CALLOWAY: Death's at the bottom of everything,
Martins. Leave death to the professionals.
```

Scenes are short. The effect is a fast pace, driving the action on, gripping the audience. Only in the two longer, unhappy scenes between Holly and Anna is the pace relaxed, but the dialogue is still clipped, terse.

HUMOUR

Humour, wit and irony flicker lightly through the dialogue and action: the taxi ride, the parrot, Paine's admiration of Holly's Westerns. Holly's mispronunciation of names: 'Winkle' and 'Callaghan' are recognisable as schoolboyish humour, quite in character, as is his tipsy chanting of 'Come out, come out, whoever you are'. The humour relieves the tension momentarily, only to trigger further suspense.

The cool wit of Lime's 'tempting' speeches points up dramatically the ruthlessness of his actions.

Irony

Greene's amused irony runs through the screenplay like a thread. Examples of different kinds are:

- the oddness of the deadly trio of Kurz, Winkel, Popescu
- Calloway's sardonic treatment of Holly
- the merciless portrait of Crabbin
- Lime's irony (detached, witty, pitiless)

Greene's screenplay is reinforced by Reed in the off-hand irony of the narrator's introduction; and by small ironic visual touches in the detail of the action:

style   mise-en-scène

bizarrely out of place

- Holly walks under a ladder on his first appearance in Vienna
- Crabbin's unacknowledged mistress
- Anna's kitten
- Kurz and the greedy diner

The grotesque

Ironic but also grotesque is the sudden introduction of everyday, innocent people into the action. The effect is funny but sinister:

- the actors in the play at the Josefstadt Theatre
- the child Hansl
- the taxi driver
- the balloon man

These appearances worry us because, although the people are quite ordinary, they seem bizarrely out of place. They suggest to us that things are out of kilter, may get worse.

mise-en-scène

Like a number of film terms, particularly those imported from France, mise-en-scène can have several severely different meanings. In this book, it is used to mean the *components of shots*. That is to say, everything that is to be recorded by the camera and microphone (as distinct from the actual *recording* of those components on film).

This review of the mise-en-scène of *The Third Man* looks at the contribution to style of three groups of skills:

- setting (and design)
- lighting
- performance (action and acting)

For ease of reading, performance is given a main heading to itself.

mise-en-scène style

> contrasts of scale

SETTING

The Vienna we see in *The Third Man* is the real city. Most exterior scenes were filmed on location. The visual feel is that of a documentary. But it is an unreal view of the city, the selective vision that the writer, the director, the designer have of the Vienna of the story.

The locations selected for *The Third Man* reflect a grim and uncertain period in the history of the city. The appearance of the squares, buildings, streets, the dramatic settings of the film's climax – the Prater Wheel, the main sewer, the Central Cemetery – reflects the tension, threats, and fears of the characters. They show us an anxious, damaged world.

Most exterior shots show damage in contrast to classical beauty and past grandeur. Elegant façades and baroque statuary are pockmarked by bombs and shells. Shattered buildings and the scaffolding of repair work are evident in many shots. A lost world of great order and aspiration is constantly juxtaposed with the reality of the effects of war.

The bleakness of the streets outside is reflected in the dreariness of the interiors: Anna's draughty flat, Winkel's fussy surgery, Calloway's basic office at police headquarters, the garish Casanova Club, the station and the hospital. Only the absent Harry's flat is spacious and comfortable.

Staircases are a prominent motif, broad and grand (to Lime's flat and to police headquarters) or narrow and confining (Anna's flat, the Cultural Centre, the sewer stairs).

The sewers, grandiose in design and unmarked by war, combine both the fleetingly lit menace of the streets with the coldness of the interior scenes. We are lost in a maze of intersecting tunnels. Even in this dark world, Reed finds striking contrasts of scale. The huge arch and main channel contrast with the very narrow, tight tunnels and the tiny stair in which Lime meets his end.

Design

At this distance in time it is hard to know how much of this skilful selection of the exteriors and atmosphere of the interiors was due to Reed, how much to his Art Director, Vincent Korda. Vincent, like his brother Alex, 'knew

style

mise-en-scène

memorable compositions

the old Vienna before the war'. What is certain is that they shared a vision of the required style.

A tribute to Korda's skill is his matching of studio design with location shots. All interiors were filmed in London. A number of exteriors (Lime hiding in the doorway, the final café, parts of streets) also had to be filmed in the studio in London, as well most of the shots of Lime in the sewers.

It is very hard for the viewer to detect the difference between film set and location; and the studio's 'Viennese' interiors are extremely convincing in their meticulous re-creation, from many still shots taken earlier, of the originals in Vienna.

LIGHTING

Recall Greene's remark that there were no 'black' or 'white' characters in his fiction, 'only black and grey'. The lighting style matches the story.

Reed and his cinematographer Robert Krasker exploit the possibilities of lighting in black-and-white film to the maximum. *Chiaroscuro* best describes the predominant style. The word (the literal meaning is 'bright-dark' in the Italian) is used here to mean images which rely for their effect on the gradations between light and darkness.

Extreme *chiaroscuro* effects are most noticeable in the night-time action in the streets and in the sewers. Light illuminates brightly only a fraction of the scene: most of the frame is composed of black and a range of greys, in silhouette and shadow. Light is used to reflect coldly off wet, empty streets, throwing elongated and menacing shadows, half-illuminating silent, watching faces. The light usually comes from an unseen source and from unnatural angles.

The management of light in these night scenes is part of the unique style and identity of the film. The effect is of mystery, danger, fear of the unknown.

Two of many high points of these memorable compositions in light are:

■ Our first sight of Lime in the doorway – the ingenious mix of half-light, shadows and darkness, then the sudden spotlight effect on his face, then the running grotesque shadow.

mise-en-scène　　　　　　　　　　　　　style

masterpiece of composition

■ Lime's last entrance: the emergence from darkness on rubble high above the street, the devil surveying his ruined world, clothed in black, partly in shadow, light hinting at his features.

In the daylight scenes, light is captured and deployed in a different way. The flat, sunless wintry light reveals the damaged city in a range of greys. The effect is of exhaustion and loss. The long final shot of the cemetery avenue, the bare trees, the still figure awaiting the distant figure, is a masterpiece of formal composition in a range of grey tones.

The lighting of the interiors varies with the action, as well as with place. Sharp contrasts between light on faces and surrounding shadow are used in scenes between Holly and Calloway. Grey shadows and muted highlights predominate for the scenes between Holly and Anna. Bright, cold lighting is used for the Casanova Club and the Cultural Centre, glaring, cold light and stark shadows in the café where Holly awaits Lime to betray him.

performance

The acting in *The Third Man*, from stars to support roles, is outstanding. Each of the actors contributes to, seems somehow to be at home in, the strange atmosphere of the film.

JOSEPH COTTEN

Cotten is the star of *The Third Man*, rightly leading the list of credits. Of the 104 minutes of the film, Cotten is in the frame for ninety-six.

Holly is a difficult part for any actor; and in a number of ways it is an unattractive role for a star. Yet Cotten keeps us fascinated from beginning to end as he blunders on with his simple-minded determination to get to the bottom of Lime's death, then to avenge him, then to betray him. There are flashes of charm in that doggedness which almost appeal to Anna, almost to Calloway, and certainly appeal to the audience.

Cotten brings to the role an occasional sweetness of character, a self-understanding, in which something better than Holly's habitual nature is revealed:

style   performance

professional maturity

■ In Anna's flat (Scene 94): Anna laughs. Holly in close-up says, disarmingly, 'I haven't seen you laugh before. Do it again. I like it'.

■ With Lime in the Wheel (Scene 116): Holly says, almost coyly, with self-awareness, 'I should be pretty easy to get rid of'.

■ With Lime at the end (Scene 137): a moving glimpse of sadness, love and compassion in Holly's last look at his old friend, as Lime nods for him to shoot and finish it.

There is in Cotten's reading of the role no effort to glamorise Holly, to give him a heroic air that the part will not sustain. He is true to Greene and Reed in this. It is a tribute to Cotten's professional maturity (this was a part not of his choosing) that his performance grips and worries us throughout. Cotten leads the narrative constantly, dragging us willingly into ever darker dilemmas.

Cotten and Welles: Orson Welles and Joseph Cotten first met as young actors in a radio series in 1934 and became friendly. They acted together frequently in Welles's Mercury Theatre, in *Citizen Kane, The Magnificent Ambersons, Journey into Fear,* and interacted well. Although Cotten was ten years older than Welles, he seemed in his roles always to be the younger man, in awe of the dominant force of the Welles character. In *The Third Man,* the roles of Holly and Lime fit this model perfectly.

ORSON WELLES

Welles's portrayal of Harry Lime lasts just ten minutes in all, and is one of the great acting performances of cinema. If his masterpiece of direction was *Citizen Kane, The Third Man* is Welles's triumph as film actor. He brings to life electrifyingly the charm, wit and truly evil heart of Lime. The greatness of the performance lies in Welles's ready understanding of the nature of Lime and in his command of dialogue and subtle facial expression.

Expression

Our first view of Lime (in the doorway opposite Anna's flat) is a classic of acting control and subtlety. The face suddenly caught in the light changes

performance

style

imploring a merciful death

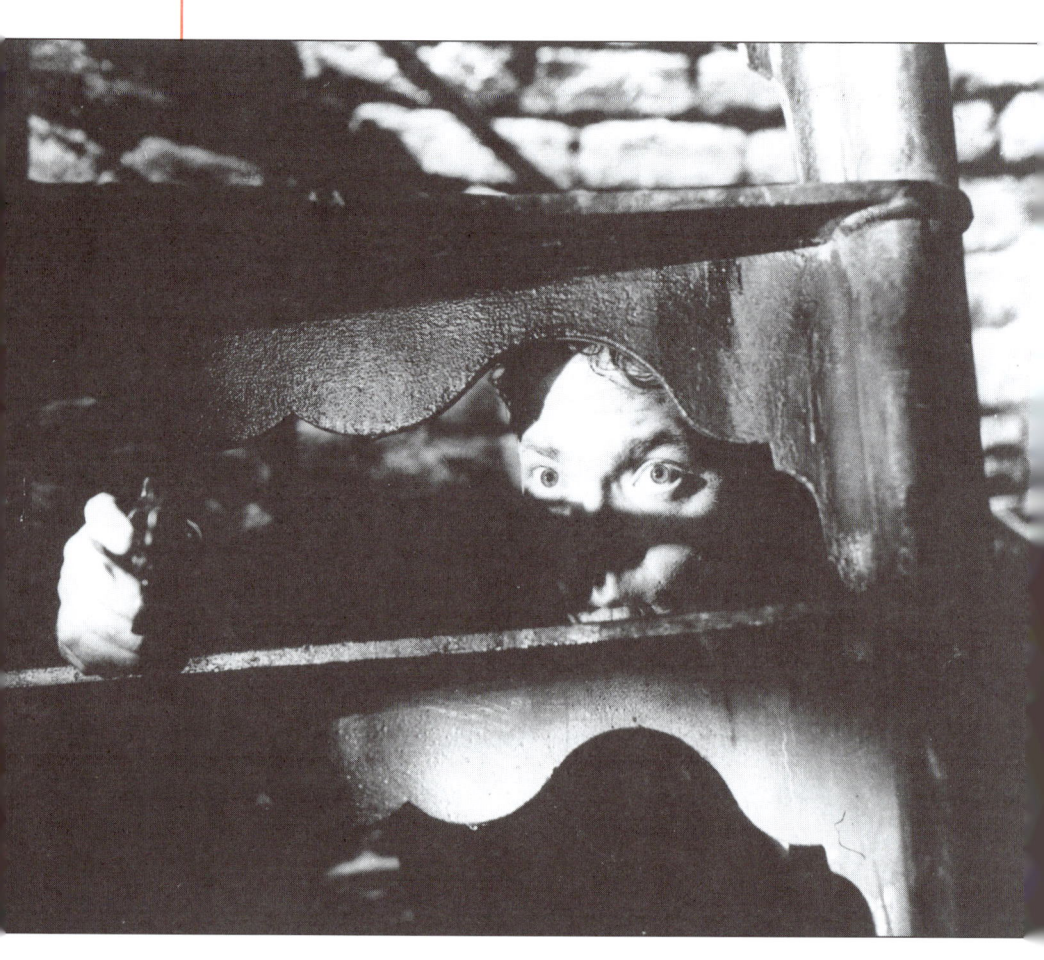

The trap closes

THE THIRD MAN

style performance

mastery of expression

rapidly: from immobility, to dangerous alertness, to faintly mischievous complicity.

Lime's entrance to the Wheel scene is jaunty, brimming confidence, one old school-chum meeting another after a gap of nine years. As the Wheel ascends, the genial confidence does not falter, but we see in the close-ups the restless eyes of the practised evader – 'What can *I* do, old man?' – and, fleetingly, the willingness to kill.

When Lime learns that the police have discovered Harbin's body in place of his own, we see suddenly the cold eyes of Mephistopheles. But his expression changes in an instant as he turns to face Holly, realising that there is no longer any point in killing him – 'What fools we are, Holly, talking like this'.

Our last view is of Lime as cornered animal, badly wounded, terrified eyes awaiting his pursuers. Holly arrives, searching Lime's face sadly for a signal, as he always has. Lime returns the stare, his eyes now beyond good and evil, imploring a merciful death rather than captivity. He nods slightly, enough for Holly and the audience. In the tunnel beyond we hear the shot.

Dialogue

Welles's mastery of facial expression is matched by his command of the dialogue. Examples of his skill can be seen in his use of *interruption* and *invention*.

Interruption – half a dozen times, Welles responds to one of Cotten's points by interrupting him, just overlapping his closing words. This is a man with more pressing things on his mind than Holly's agonisings about right and wrong. Lime controls the dialogue and Holly, and the scene.

Invention – Welles's pro-active style included changes to the dialogue on the set. In *The Third Man* they are few but characteristic.

In the Great Wheel sequence Welles improvised two small additions to the script: 'There's no proof against me, besides you' and a brief sequence about indigestion, 'These are the only thing that helps, these tablets ...'

performance   style

dramatic effect

His third invention, the entire 'cuckoo-clock' speech, proved memorable:

```
'When you make up your mind, send me a message –
I'll meet you any place, any time, and when we do
meet, old man, it's you I want to see, not the
police ... and don't be so gloomy ... after all,
it's not that awful – you know what the fellow said
... In Italy for thirty years under the Borgias they
had warfare, terror, murder, bloodshed – they
produced Michelangelo, Leonardo da Vinci and the
Renaissance. In Switzerland they had brotherly love,
five hundred years of democracy and peace, and what
did that produce ...? The cuckoo clock. So long,
Holly.'
```

This witty exit speech is completely in tune with the character of Lime and with Greene's screenplay. Greene himself later acknowledged the dramatic effect, generously calling it 'the best line in the film'.

TREVOR HOWARD

If Welles *is* Lime, Howard *is* Calloway ('whom I see now always in my mind with the features of Trevor Howard', Greene wrote later).

Calloway was a relatively early role in Howard's career (he jumped to fame in *Brief Encounter* in 1945) but he reveals himself in *The Third Man* as an accomplished, professionally mature actor. Perhaps it was a bonus that he had been a British army officer during the war: he had no difficulty assuming the military rank and manner required for the part.

Greene wrote Calloway as a policeman seconded into the army. Howard's performance combines soldier and policeman, suggesting a man with long experience of both war and crime. Howard's features, expression and body language combine to show a man with no illusions, in command of his job: a man of few words, entirely focused on the present task, decisive, competent, unsentimental.

Howard's clipped speech perfectly matches Greene's dialogue, as his ironic manner matches the understatement of Reed's style. His timing of lines

style — performance

personal experience of war

(for example, in his opening words, 'Fellow called Lime', and the pause before his response to Holly's question about the price Calloway would pay for co-operation – 'Name it') is masterly.

Howard shows us the unsympathetic side of Calloway's single-mindedness (a ruthlessness and manipulation worthy of Lime), yet suggests an underlying humanity and a passion for justice without once talking of them.

ALIDA VALLI

Much of Valli's performance as Anna is necessarily low-key, muted and resigned in her grief for Harry. After Lime's 'resurrection' she reveals the strength and fire of Anna's character, a principled courage which surpasses that of Lime, Holly or Calloway.

Valli brings to the role welcome touches of warmth which give the character depth:

■ When the International Patrol searches Anna's flat (Scene 37) the landlady complains loudly and continually in German, irritating everyone except Anna. Kindness and understanding of her landlady's troubles illuminate her face as she tells Holly, 'It's her house. Give her some cigarettes'.

■ Anna's surprising laugh, at Holly's absurdity (Scene 94); for the first and only time her face and posture suddenly seem that of a young woman.

■ Anna's passionate contempt as she rejects her safe passage and Holly at the railway station (Scene 120): 'Look at yourself in the window – they have a name for faces like that ...'.

Valli shared with all the other actors (except the two Americans) personal experience of war and hard life in Europe during the 1940s, and she conveys implicitly something of that knowledge in her portrayal of Anna. Wariness, loss and endurance are present throughout the performance.

Valli makes her exit, the long walk out of the story, with a fatalism and grace worthy of Garbo.

performance   style

small but vital roles

THE AUSTRIANS

The Third Man owes much of its atmosphere and 'documentary' immediacy to Reed's casting of Viennese film actors. These are small but vital roles: all the performances are accomplished and memorable.

Ernst Deutsch (Kurz), gives the 'Baron' a faded elegance, criminality evident behind the ingratiating eyes. The contrast between Holly's dogged questions and the apologetic evasion of Kurz is beautifully acted. Deutsch was a veteran of the stage in Germany and the USA, and acted in sixty-one films.

Erich Ponto (Dr Winkel) provides the doctor with a bogus respectability. He makes the wordplay with Holly ('Dr Winkle?') both amusing and menacing. His strange partnership with Kurz fascinates. Ponto was another experienced actor, with more than fifty film credits.

Siegfried Breuer (Popescu) in contrast gives us a small-time serious gangster, nattily dressed and dangerous, in severe contrast to the genteel villainy of his associates. Breuer was a film director and acted in some thirty films.

Paul Hoerbiger (Porter) knew no English and learned the part phonetically. He is every inch the frightened but decent man who does not want to be involved, and his famous line, 'There was a third man' is delivered with just the right emphasis. Hoerbiger acted in more than 245 films.

Hedwig Bleibtrau (Anna's landlady), speaking only in German, adds another 'off-beat' touch to the film. Her outrage at the invasion of her house by the police, the shrieking harsh voice of protest, adds a nightmarish touch. Bleibtrau was a famous stage actress in Vienna and starred in some twenty films.

Herbert Halbik (Hansl) – Reed's genius for eliciting convincing performance from children contrives to make this toddler surreal: both innocent and sinister.

ENGLISH SUPPORT

Bernard Lee is quite at home in the role of the competent Sergeant Paine, stalwart sidekick of Calloway. Lee shows that Paine knows his rank and his style   camera and sound

understatement

job as a thoroughly experienced professional; and delivers the running gag of his admiration for Holly's Westerns with nicely judged understatement.

Wilfrid Hyde-White as Crabbin of the Cultural Centre provides expert comic relief of a different kind, a flash of absurdity in the action. The fussy, self-absorbed role is a world apart from Lime's Vienna: and another example of comedy adding to the out-of-kilter atmosphere of *The Third Man*.

Both Lee and Hyde-White played many comparable roles with confident expertise in their long careers in British films.

ACTION

The style of the physical action in *The Third Man* is one of understatement. The exception is the climax of the film, a masterly, breathless manhunt in the maze of the sewers.

Violence is consistently understated. We experience the porter's murder only by the sudden fear in his face. Harbin's death is not seen, Lime's death is not seen. Paine collapses tidily and silently. The black market is a palpable presence, but never seen. In the children's ward we are not shown the victims, only the momentary shot of a no-longer-needed teddy-bear.

Love and sex are also understated. Although Reed cunningly suggests to the audience the growth of a romance between Holly and Anna – so much so that their final parting is poignant – the two 'lovers' in fact do not embrace, kiss, or even touch throughout the film.

Understatement is a stylistic preference of Reed's: a belief that the effects of passion, violence and evil can be more vivid and convincing on the screen when their physical action is implied, left to the imagination.

camera and sound

CINEMATOGRAPHY

Robert Krasker had worked as cinematographer with Reed on *Odd Man Out* (1947) and with David Lean on *Brief Encounter* (1946). In both films he used some of the techniques of lighting and camerawork which were deployed more spectacularly in *The Third Man*.

camera and sound   style

distorted views

Reed was in no doubt of the visual effects he wished to achieve. Together, lighting and camera define a large part of the style of the film.

Angles

Characters, action and background in *The Third Man* are frequently seen by the camera and the audience (only occasionally by the characters) at an 'unnatural' angle. Three techniques, producing different kinds of angles, are used, either singly or in combination:

■ The camera is tilted to one side: the most noticeable and unsettling technique. It sends signals of unease: everything in vision seems out of kilter.

■ The camera is positioned at an oblique angle to the left or right of the action.

■ The camera is positioned below or above the subject, altering subtly or extremely our superior or inferior view of the scene or character. Upward shots of Harry Lime, and of staircases, recur. Even the worrying face of the small child Hansl is viewed more than once from ground level.

Another angular effect of a different kind is produced through the use of a wide-angle lens, mainly for exteriors. Apart from its advantage of catching a wider sweep of characters or setting, it also distorts subtly everything in the frame.

Expressionist effect

These techniques are not unlike those of the German 'expressionist' cinema of the 1920s. In combination with artful lighting (which produces unnatural highlights and shadows from odd angles), they produce a distorted view, striking images at moments of suspense, danger or anxiety. The effect is both arresting and disturbing.

One of many examples is shown in the still on page 17. Lime keeps his final appointment. The frame is tilted ten degrees to the left, the camera looks up at him from floor level, slightly oblique. Strong light from three directions and unrealistic angles reveals both the stark, 'crooked' shadow of the door and the pale moon of Lime's face staring from a channel of darkness.

style — camera and sound

subtle contribution

The 'expressionist' effects tend to predominate in the memory, but they occupy less than half the time of the film.

Long and short

Other, more conventional techniques are deployed, no less memorably:

- Close-ups: the contrasting close-ups of Holly with Kurz and with Winkel; of Holly and Lime in the Great Wheel; of Lime's desperate fingers; and the magnificent final close-up of Lime.
- Long shots: the superb high vertical shot in the Wheel, looking down on people as ants; the high and distant shot of the conspirators on the bridge; and the astonishing final shot of the film, the stationary camera recording Anna's walk towards it from extreme long shot to extreme close-up and beyond. The shot lasts one and a half minutes.

SOUND

The dialogue and music may dominate in the impact of the sound of *The Third Man*, but other sounds contribute subtly to the story and style.

Sounds heard in a film which originate directly from *within* the film's story are sometimes called *diegetic*, in contrast to *non-diegetic* sounds which are heard by the audience but not by any of the characters.

In *The Third Man*, the blasé introductory voice-over, 'Oh wait, I was going to tell you ...' – and, of course, the zither music throughout, are both *non-diegetic*. Each speaks to the audience directly and plays the role of narrator, chorus or commentator. Detached from the action, they influence our reactions strongly, unheard and unnoticed by the characters.

Spoken dialogue is obviously the diegetic sound of first importance, both to story and style. But the sounds of the action within the story, the way they are selected, recorded and edited, follow close in shaping the style of the film. A few examples of the subtle contribution of sound to the style of *The Third Man* are given below:

- The Viennese characters speaking German, except to Holly – part documentary style, part alienating effect.

camera and sound   style

unseen character

- The night sounds, the heightened echo of the crash of boots running through deserted streets and sewers – heighten tension, anxiety.
- The thin keening sound of the wind as Lime's fingers reach in vain through the sewer grating – timeless and eerie.
- The echoing shouts of unseen police in the maze of the sewers – bewildering Lime, heightening tension.

music

Music plays an exceptional part in *The Third Man*. One instrument, the zither, its music composed, improvised and performed by one man, Anton Karas, is heard throughout the film. There is no other music.

The zither is a many-stringed instrument, part of the popular tradition of folk and café music in Austria and central Europe. Its sound is not unlike that of a guitar, but its timbre and range are immediately distinctive to the ear: sometimes jangly, with deep reverberating bass, sometimes delicate and lilting.

Reed first heard the zither in the background at a welcome party for the film crew in Vienna. Fascinated by the sound, he tracked down the performer, Anton Karas, whose usual work was to play in a wine-bar in the suburbs. Karas was a modest performer, the Viennese equivalent of a cocktail pianist, and could barely read music. Reed was so taken with the effect of his music, its 'rightness' for the story and action, that he decided to use the zither to accompany the entire film.

Later, in London at the sound-editing stage, Reed spent many evenings with Karas as he played over the images on screen, monitoring every second of the recording, coaxing and suggesting the effect he wanted for each scene. In a sense, the resultant sound and film score are as much Reed's as Karas's.

We hear the music of the 'Harry Lime theme' as the film opens. We see the strings of the zither vibrating, forming an abstract composition behind the credits.

With that calling card, the music quickly establishes itself as an unseen character in the film. This character in part seems to be an interpreter

style — editing

unique effect

of the story for the audience, in part a citizen of Vienna commenting wryly on the action.

The Harry Lime theme is an unambitious little tune, barely a melody, built from a repetition of three notes, a simple chord progression and a few variations. The theme is played complete at first, and recurs in parts throughout the film, especially when Lime's presence is suspected or real. The zither enters with numerous other brief improvisations during the action, some mischievous, some warning, some passionate, some melancholy.

The unique effect of the music, and its indelible stamp on the film text and style of *The Third Man* is difficult to capture in words. Each listener and viewer experiences this somewhat differently, of course. Beyond doubt, the music establishes a strong mood or atmosphere, but how to sum it up?

There is only a rough consensus among critics about what that mood might be: 'wistful' (Paul Driver, *Sight and Sound*), 'both jaunty and ominous' (AQ in *The Independent*), 'plaintive' (Tom Dawson, *Total Film*), 'jaunty but without joy, like whistling in the dark' (Roger Ebert, *Chicago Sun-Times*), 'melancholy heightened by haunting, relentless zither music' (Georges Sadoul). Perhaps it is all of these.

Compare the theme with Kurt Weill's 'Mack the Knife' in *The Threepenny Opera*. Initially, any resemblance of tune and style might seem far-fetched. But they have two things in common: a simple repetitive three-note motif and a native son's view of the underworld in a capital city devastated by war (Berlin, 1928 and Vienna, 1948). Both contrive to be mocking, defiant, romantic, melancholy, streetwise. The 'atmosphere' of the two tunes, and of the stories they illustrate are not far apart.

The zither music made a wholly unprecedented impact on critics, public and the music industry when *The Third Man* opened in London (see Contexts, Zither fever).

editing

Reed's editor for *The Third Man* was Oswald Hafenrichter. The two had worked together the year before on *The Fallen Idol*. Hafenrichter was an

editing

style

unseen art

Austrian, resident in England since the early days of the war, an editor of long experience who had worked in the UFA studios in the 1930s. He received an Oscar nomination for his work on *The Third Man*.

Editing is the unseen art of film. The quality of the partnership of director and editor is critical to the result. How much of the final effect of *The Third Man* is due to Reed, how much to Hafenrichter? It is impossible for anyone not directly involved to know. Here are some examples of the results of their work:

CONTINUITY

Pace

The Third Man starts as it means to go on. The introductory voice-over of the narrator is brisk as he sets the scene of occupied Vienna. As he talks, we see a rapid montage of about thirty documentary shots of Vienna, moving from elegant buildings and statuary to bombed rubble, to beggars, low-life black marketeers, a body in the river's ooze, shots of the international patrol. The last of these dissolves into the railway station and the expectant face of Holly Martins as he arrives. All of this has lasted just 1 minute 8 seconds.

The sequence from that point to the shot of Holly staring speechless at Harry's grave, takes less than two minutes of film time.

The pace of the unfolding of the story is fast. There is no padding, each short scene opens new doors to the mystery. We have barely grasped a scene's import before it cuts sharply to the next new face, new action, new setting.

Rhythm

If *The Third Man* were simply a thriller or 'action movie', it might be appropriate for the opening pace to be kept up throughout. But we have seen that the thriller is interleaved with a more reflective story of love and betrayal. There is a rhythm of contrasting pace and styles. The three scenes in which Holly is alone with Anna have a slower pace, to match Anna's unhappiness and Holly's growing infatuation. The momentous dialogue between Holly and Lime in the Great Wheel, isolated from the complexities

style editing

momentous dialogue

'Don't try to be a
policeman, old man'

THE THIRD MAN

editing   style

tension provided by the plot

below, is calm: the tension is provided by the plot and by the slow climb and fall of their cabin. Each of these slower sequences dissolves into the fast pace of the next action in the thriller.

TECHNIQUES

Cutting

The dominant editing technique used in *The Third Man* is razor-sharp cutting from shot to shot and from scene to scene. There are few dissolves and even fewer tracking shots.

Consider the style and editing of one of the most famous sequences: Holly's discovery that Lime is alive (scene 95).

In the street, by accident, Holly is amazed to see Lime standing in the shadow of a doorway.

> The moment when the light hits his face is one of the most exquisitely twisted, dementedly cool moments in cinema.
>
> *Andrew O'Hagan, Daily Telegraph, 1999*

In fact, there are three rapid close-up shots of Lime's face, intercut with reversed shots of the astonished Holly, though in our memory they stay as one. By the time he runs across the road Lime has disappeared, like magic. Holly hears running footsteps, chases the shadow and sound into an empty square, but Lime has disappeared. The whole sequence is made up of thirty shots and lasts only 1 minute 45 seconds. The effect is breathtaking.

Montage

There are two outstanding examples of the use of stylish montage to drive up the tension:

■ After the porter's murder, the rapid series of close-ups of gaunt faces in the crowd outside as their concern turns to suspicion

■ As the police stand hidden, waiting for Lime's appearance, the succession of close-ups of alert faces, plumes of breath in the frosty night air, intercut with the heads of blind statues.

style | a unique style

difficult to capture

a unique style

'Strangely off-beat' was Bosley Crowther's phrase for it. The overall style of *The Third Man* may be individual and striking, but it is difficult to capture in a phrase. For fifty years, critics and viewers have struggled to sum it up. What their impressions have in common is the appreciation of a powerful mood or atmosphere that envelops the story. But what sort of mood is it that Reed has created?

> Dream-like quality that follows Holly's disorientating journey to its dramatic conclusion
>
> *Anwar Brett, Film Review, 1999*

> A pungent atmosphere of decay and corruption suffuses
>
> *Tom Dawson, Total Film, 1999*

> An overwhelmingly melancholic atmosphere
>
> *Georges Sadoul, quoted by Film Unlimited website*

> The film's disenchanted romanticism exerts an irresistible charm
>
> *Philip Kemp, Sight and Sound, 1994*

> Weary and knowing, its glorious style was an act of defiance against the corrupt world it pictured
>
> *Roger Ebert, Chicago Sun-Times, 1999*

These varying impressions have in common the suggestion of world-weariness. Yet the experience of watching the film is tense, exciting, involving, amusing. The 'mood' and subtext perhaps have a delayed action, become alive after the final shot and persist in the memory after the event.

OVERALL EFFECT

A strong feature of *The Third Man*, as of other great films, is the fusion of the narrative content with its style.

The efforts to define the overall effect of the film and its style have included occasionally the terms *romantic* or *expressionist*, even *existential*.

a unique style

'Mischievous tragi-comedy'

The last of these might mean many things and will not be pursued here, but something of the first two can certainly be seen in *The Third Man*.

Holly's doomed courtship of Anna, Anna's unswerving passion for Lime, the poignancy of the final shot, all these are certainly romantic in style. In a different sense, the stylistic treatment of Lime, part Byronic hero, part Mephistopheles, part gangster, might be called romantic.

We have seen that a strong part of the lighting and camera work in *The Third Man* is reminiscent of German 'expressionist' films such as *The Cabinet of Dr Caligari* (1919). In these early silent films distorted sets, strong lighting contrasts, angles, shadows, evoked a threatening, unreal world seen in a dark mood of mental anguish or paranoia. Certainly Reed made conscious use of a number of 'expressionist' effects to match pessimistic and fearful threads in *The Third Man*. But his thriller never departs from realistic fiction, a world apart from that of expressionist cinema.

In the end the film will not bear either romanticism or expressionism as its dominant style. The 'grim grin' of the authors, Greene and Reed, keeps breaking through.

A 'Mischievous tragi-comedy' (AQ in *The Independent*, 1999) is perhaps the closest that anyone has come to an appropriate category for *The Third Man* and its style.

The Viennese (fittingly) have an old saying, 'The situation is hopeless but not serious'. That might also serve as an echo of the style, of the story, and of the film itself.

contexts

writing The Third Man *p65*   making The Third Man *p69*
the audience *p74*   ideologies *p76*   cultural *p79*   cinematic *p83*
influence *p87*   evaluation *p90*

writing the third man

It is very uncommon for a well-known novelist to be commissioned to write an original screenplay and then to work closely and successfully with the director to the completion of the film. The evolution of *The Third Man* from jotting to 'final' screenplay provides a revealing insight into the contexts of the film.

Sometime in 1947, somewhere in his travels, Graham Greene scribbled an idea for the opening of a story on the back of an envelope:

> I had paid my last farewell to Harry a week ago, when his coffin was lowered into the frozen February ground, so that it was with incredulity that I saw him pass by, without a sign of recognition, among the host of strangers in the Strand.

In September 1947, Greene wrote to his lover, Catherine Walston:

> The act of creation is awfully odd and inexplicable like falling in love ... all the ideas I had – the first sentence of the thriller about the dead Harry who wasn't dead, the Risen-from-the-dead story, and then the other day in the train all seemed to come together. I hope to God it lasts – they don't always ...

In December 1947, Greene was asked to dinner by Alexander Korda and Carol Reed. They talked about their recently completed *The Fallen Idol*. Korda said that he wanted to work with Greene again, this time with an original screenplay rather than an adaptation. Reed would produce and direct.

writing the third man — contexts

first treatment

Greene, with nothing else to offer, outlined his sketch of an 'entertainment' about 'risen-from-the-dead' Harry and its possible development as a thriller.

Korda was taken with the idea, but wanted a story set in post-war Vienna, where he had lived and worked as film director when a young man. He was struck by reports from friends of the damage and hard times of the occupied city.

Greene accepted a contract with London Films in January 1948 to write 'an original story suitable for production of a cinematograph film'.

WRITING THE NOVEL

There are two authorised texts of *The Third Man*, both by Graham Greene – the novel and the screenplay of the film. Greene wrote the novel as the first stage of writing the screenplay. He called it a 'first treatment':

> To me it is almost impossible to write a film play without first writing a story ... cannot make the first act of creation in script form.

In February 1948, Greene visited 'the smashed, dreary city of Vienna' for two weeks, in search of a plot to flesh out the idea of his 'dead Harry who wasn't dead'. From contacts made through Korda and British Intelligence, he learned about the deadly racket of stealing penicillin from hospitals, and about the extraordinary sewer system of Vienna – and its use by agents to travel unchecked between the four occupied zones of the city.

Greene started to sketch his story, 'I had my film'. Greene then went to Italy to write the novel (or 'treatment'). He finished it by the end of April, 1948.

WRITING THE SCREENPLAY

In June 1948, Greene returned to Vienna, this time with Carol Reed, to start work on the screenplay. They stayed for twenty days of hard writing, late nights and hard drinking. In his later preface to the novel, Greene recalled:

> On these treatments Carol Reed and I worked closely together, covering so many feet of carpet a day, acting scenes at each other. No third ever joined our conferences ...

contexts — writing the third man

triumph of stonewalling

By early July, the first draft of the screenplay was finished, and by the end of August 1948, Greene and Reed finished the second draft of the screenplay in London. The 'final' screenplay was completed by the end of September, almost to the point of the shooting script. Filming was to start in Vienna in October, 1948.

THE SELZNICK FACTOR

Alexander Korda needed David O. Selznick to co-produce *The Third Man*, to secure investment and American distribution. In May 1948, on Selznick's yacht in Bermuda, Korda and Reed discussed the 'first treatment' with Selznick; and the co-producing contract was signed days later.

For the next six months, right up to the start of filming in Vienna, Selznick bombarded Korda and Reed with cables, letters, emissaries, suggesting and demanding many changes to the screenplay.

In August, Reed and Greene travelled to California and endured a week of close discussion of the first draft screenplay with Selznick. Greene refers to this series of meetings as a kind of triumph of stonewalling by Reed, with no concessions made ('Graham and I will think about it'). But Selznick's bombardment was only just beginning.

Many of Selznick's wide range of demands boiled down to wanting to boost the 'American image' in the film. For example, he was incensed at what he saw as the film's presentation of British dominance in Vienna. An example of dozens of crass judgements was that he thought the film's title useless for the box office, and suggested 'Night in Vienna'.

Most of Selznick's ideas and detailed demands were not acted upon; and no doubt most were absurd to British eyes. The transatlantic frustration grew to a dangerous level. Only the practised urbanity of Korda and evasive diplomacy of Reed saved the screenplay and *The Third Man* as a joint production; but Selznick withdrew his commitment to future co-productions.

Two major contributions

Some of Selznick's proposals were adopted. Two of them are vital to the final film text – in fact, to the opening and closing shots.

writing the third man   contexts

major disputes

The narrative introduction: It was Selznick who suggested a change to the original opening montage of Holly's journey across the Atlantic and Europe. A montage of present-day Vienna, with voice-over narration, would provide the viewer with a crisp introduction to the complicated city. Reed admired this idea and put together the montage and voice-over in post-production at Shepperton, with the results that we know.

The final scene: The most surprising and most important Selznick suggestion concerned the final scene of the 'treatment'. In Greene's novel, Rollo (Holly) catches up with Anna as she leaves the cemetery. Before they turn out of Calloway's sight, 'her hand was through his arm'.

Greene wrote later:

> One of the very few major disputes between Carol Reed and myself concerned the ending, and he has been proved triumphantly right. I held the view that an entertainment of this kind was too light an affair to carry the weight of an unhappy ending ... I had not given enough consideration to the mastery of Reed's direction.

But in his notes of the early Bermuda conference between Korda, Selznick and Reed (Greene was not present), Reed records:

> Selznick felt that it was a great pity that at the end of the story Rollo and the girl Anna should finish together; we should go from the cemetery scene to Anna going away by herself.

It is probable that Reed initially was also of that opinion and needed no convincing; and in his subsequent discussions with Greene thought it counter-productive to mention Selznick.

The real irony of this is that Greene (of all writers) should first draft a 'happy' ending in the interests of box-office appeal to such a relentlessly unhappy fable as *The Third Man;* and that Selznick (of all producers) should see that this would be false.

DIRECTOR AND SCRIPT

The 'final' version of the screenplay is the result of Greene's writing and rewriting with the close participation of Reed. The Faber edition

contexts — making the third man

unrecorded variations

(which carries the personal endorsement of both Greene and Reed) gives a fascinating insight into the writing of the last three drafts of the 'final script'. We can see the many cuts and alterations made by Greene and Reed in the *second draft* and in the *shooting script*, and by Reed during *filming*.

Many small changes were made on location or set, devised by Reed or the actors. Yet even this 'final' printed version does not always correspond exactly with what is said and seen on screen. There are many tiny unrecorded variations, one or two of them significant. For example, the script shows Anna's line about her kitten (who was to betray Lime's presence to Holly) as 'he only likes cats'. In the scene, we hear 'he only liked Harry', a brilliant after-thought by Reed.

making the third man

THE STARS

Holly and Lime were Englishmen in Greene's original story. Hollywood stars for at least these roles were an important part of the Korda-Selznick agreement. Initially in considering possible players, Korda, Reed and Selznick stayed with Englishmen. Cary Grant and Noel Coward were the first proposals for Holly and Lime. Grant was not enthusiastic, the search was widened. The possibility of Lime and Holly as Canadians or Americans was now entertained.

David Niven, James Stewart, Robert Mitchum, Robert Taylor, Barbara Stanwyck were among the names considered for the film, with varying degrees of realism. Reed and Korda were persistently keen to get Orson Welles to play Lime. Selznick was reluctant, believing that Welles's studio reputation in America made him almost unmarketable.

Selznick then lobbied in favour of Joseph Cotten and Alida Valli (players already under contract to him). Cotten initially was reluctant to play Holly, and Reed was initially unenthusiastic about Cotten in that role. In the end, the casting was resolved in a few months by a familiar combination of realities and compromises.

making the third man contexts

key locations

Cotten asked for his character's first name to be changed: it seemed to him to convey homosexuality. Puzzlingly, he accepted Greene's suggestion that Rollo should become Holly.

Welles was the most elusive and difficult of the stars to pin down. Attracted to the role only by the constant need for a quick fee to finance his own projects, Welles led Korda and Reed a mischievous dance across Europe before he signed up.

Reed had first wanted Ralph Richardson to play Calloway, but Richardson thought the role was overshadowed by Lime and Holly. Trevor Howard proved a better choice.

HOW THE FILM WAS MADE

Vienna

In his fortnight in Vienna looking for his story, Greene had visited the sights and the bars of the city. The locations he chose for the novel are the key locations of the film. When Greene and Reed worked on the first draft of the script in Vienna four months later, Reed was able to explore these places, the streets and the 'feel' of the city. Later still, as shooting started, Reed, his designer Vincent Korda and cinematographer Robert Krasker, selected more particularly.

Shooting started in Vienna in late October, 1948 and finished in mid-December. The Prater Wheel, the sewers, the cemetery, and many city street scenes were filmed on location. At the same time, interior scenes were meticulously researched, selected and photographed, so that interiors could be filmed later in England.

Shepperton

The division between location and studio filming was not straightforward. Orson Welles spent very little time in the real sewers: most of his performance underground was given on Shepperton sets. The all-important scene in the Wheel's cabin between Lime and Holly had to be shot in the studio. The two funerals in the cemetery, all of the interiors and even some of the street shots (part of Lime's first doorway sequence, for example) were filmed in London.

contexts   # making the third man

meticulous research

Holly and Calloway
'I never did like policemen'

making the third man — contexts

contractual disagreement

It is part of the extraordinary technical skill of *The Third Man* that the 'join' between location and studio shots of these distinctive 'foreign' settings is never noticeable: illusions created by film-making at its best.

Filming started at Shepperton in January 1949. By the end of March, the principal photography had been completed and the stars dispersed.

The English version of *The Third Man* is Reed's final cut. The American version (at least until 1999) was shorter, cut by Selznick.

The final cut

The Third Man was first shown publicly in London early in September 1949. Selznick had seen the final cut of the film a week previously, and was dazzled. Many of his earlier reservations about the script were forgotten in the warmth of the enormous public and critical success.

But contractual disagreement between Selznick and Korda welled up again, this time about the release of *The Third Man* in the USA. The dispute, about production credits, editing and profit-sharing, became fierce. Korda badly needed a financial success after several expensive flops, and found that he had a good bargaining counter in the British and Continental success of *The Third Man* (and its music); he also had the negative of the final cut.

The American version

Eventually Korda and Selznick reached agreement. *The Third Man* was released in New York early in February 1950. Selznick had insisted on editing rights.

Selznick cut the film by eleven minutes in all, in what he believed to be the interests of the American box office. No scene was removed entirely, but numerous small cuts were made to action and dialogue throughout. The cuts add up to a significant (and many would think pointless) change for the worse. Incredibly, Anna's final walk from the cemetery (which lasts ninety seconds) was cut by thirty-five seconds.

Selznick had all along badgered the British to make Holly a less unsatisfactory American, more heroic, more acceptable to the American public. He changed and shortened the already brief introduction. He

contexts | # making the third man

contrast between attitudes

substituted Cotten's (Holly's) voice for Reed's as the narrator. An important effect of this is to change the point of view of the film. The removal of the unknown 'story teller' works against the ironic detachment of the narration that watermarks the entire story. The impression given is that this will be Holly's tale, a kind of wry success story told at a later time by himself.

Ownership

The Third Man is usually thought of in the UK as a British film; but it was in fact an Anglo-American co-production, one of the first of many after the Second World War.

In May 1948, the British government initiated an Anglo-American film agreement, one of a history of efforts to bolster the ailing British industry. By virtue of that agreement, Korda and Selznick contracted to produce four films together. *The Third Man* would be the first. Korda's London Films would make the film, Reed would produce and direct. Selznick would provide two or three Hollywood stars under contract to him for the main roles, and part of the production costs, in return for rights to American distribution.

The attraction of the deal to Korda was the ability to finance and distribute the film internationally, with a major budget and instantly marketable stars. One attraction of the deal to Selznick was that it gave him the opportunity of reinvesting profits made by his films in Britain. Selznick was a strong admirer of *The Fallen Idol*. There was a good possibility of profit and of kudos in the deal for both parties in the agreement.

The contrast between the attitudes of the two men to film production was extreme. Korda's aim was to give Reed maximum independence, and negotiating support when needed. Selznick was at the opposite extreme: he wanted detailed, day-to-day control of his films.

The Third Man was produced and directed 6,000 miles from Hollywood. Despite the constant efforts of the American co-producer to make unwelcome changes from afar, the production partnership survived (just) the making of the film. *The Third Man* was completed in the UK on time and within budget, in the form that Reed wished.

Korda and Selznick made no more films together.

making the third man   contexts

the Breen office

Censorship

Apart from Selznick, Reed had to worry about the powerful 'independent' censorship used by Hollywood in this era – the Breen office. The power and scope of American film censorship in the 1940s is difficult to credit today. The Breen representatives found much to object to in the first-draft script of *The Third Man*, particularly about sex, violence and drink:

> There should be no dialogue definitely pointing up illicit sex relationship between Anna and Harry ... Americans should not be shown drunk ... There must be no scenes showing law-enforcing officers dying at the hands of criminals ...

Reed had little trouble accommodating the Breen censors. We have seen that understatement is, in any case, a conscious part of the style of *The Third Man*: the underlying passions and violence of the story gain in their impact by suggestion and allusion. But drink is essential to Greene's and Reed's vision of Holly Martins (whether English or American): he is at least a chronic tippler.

Somehow Reed got away with it. In the finished film there are few of Holly's scenes where a bottle and glass are not close to his hand, and several in which his speech is slurred and unreasonable. The fate of Sergeant Paine (undeniably a law-enforcing officer dying at the hands of criminals) is quite explicit.

The British Board of Film Censors appeared to have no difficulty with the film. They required no cuts and swiftly awarded *The Third Man* an 'A' certificate. This meant that children were allowed to see it if accompanied by an adult.

the audience

THE CINEMA AUDIENCE

The British cinema audience in 1949 was vast: there were more than 1,500 million attendances in the year. The record was set in 1946, when attendances exceeded 1,600 million. Across every social class it was by far the most popular entertainment of the time. It was common for

contexts | **the audience**

popular reputation

teenagers, adults, families to go to the cinema twice, sometimes even three times a week. The cinema and the dance-hall were the true popular entertainment of the country: both were relatively cheap, the cinema very accessible.

In addition to film critics of the press and film magazines, word of mouth spread the popularity or avoidance of a particular film fast and wide among the cinema-going millions. The power of popular reputation, as unpredictable in its favour then as now, swept *The Third Man* to huge sales in the ABC chain of cinemas; and later, in the small independents. It attracted both the mass audience and 'intellectual' audience alike.

POST-WAR PERCEPTIONS

Britain in 1949 was still exhausted and impoverished by war. It was the era of 'Austerity'. Ration books for food, clothes, fuel, introduced at the beginning of the Second World War in 1939, were still in force, compulsory for everyone. Everything material in life was regulated, had to be queued for. Cars, household gadgets, desirable goods of all kinds, were expensive and in very short supply. The emerging television service was a luxury beyond the dreams of all but a few.

How did the British audience of the time view the setting of *The Third Man*? With fascination, recognition, but scant sympathy. War-torn Vienna was shown at length with vivid realism; but Britain's cities were similarly torn. Many huge wastelands of bomb-damage were still unrestored in London, Coventry, Southampton, Bristol and other cities. The audience of 1949 was at home with the damage and the shabbiness of Vienna. But memories of the war were still powerful; and Vienna had been a city of the enemy.

The four-power military government of occupied Vienna would be curious but unsurprising to most in the audience. Virtually every man in every British audience of *The Third Man* was either serving in the army (national military service) or was an ex-soldier. Very many women of the time were ex-service or had spent years on war work in factories.

A minor fascination of *The Third Man* at the time was its 'foreignness'. It was a novelty to see a story with American and British stars in a

the audience

underlying preoccupations

'peace-time' Europe which few of the audience had seen or could visit. Foreign travel for a decade after the war was expensive and difficult, hampered by strict bureaucratic controls and battered transport systems.

British audiences during the war and for some years after would have experience of the idea and practice of a black market, but the scale and criminality of the rackets shown in Vienna would be novel. The (real-life) trade in stolen penicillin and other medical drugs revealed a harshness and desperation of existence unknown among the undefeated allies of the West.

ideologies

The entertainment of *The Third Man* contains no overt moral or political intentions or messages: the explicit intention of its makers was solely to thrill and amuse. But we have already noted (in Narrative and Form: Themes) an underlying 'subtext' with several strong moral preoccupations. Are there other implications in the film text, connections between what we see and the moral, political and social values of its time?

A FLAWED WORLD

Traditional moral beliefs and Greene's own complex Christian perceptions are part of the context of the film. Underlying preoccupations with the power of evil, scepticism about the possibility of redemption, and of the probability of betrayal are ingrained in *The Third Man*, as in most of Greene's novels.

Long before his conversion to Catholicism, 'Evil' seemed to Greene a living reality in the world. In his short essay *The Lost Childhood* he tells of his boyhood reading and the tremendous impact that reading Marjorie Bowen's novel *The Viper of Milan* made on him at the age of fourteen. Greene saw in the book and in his unhappy life at school that:

> Goodness has only once found a perfect incarnation in a human body and never will again, but evil can always find a home there. Human nature is not black and white but black and grey.

contexts

ideologies

betrayal and loss

The experience of reading the book (a thrilling historical adventure) gave him the determination to be a writer. At the same time it gave him 'the pattern' for his later work:

> Perfect evil walking the world where perfect good can never walk again, and only the pendulum ensures that after all in the end justice is done.

Betrayal

In the wake of evil, betrayal and loss are part of the human condition. Innocence is lost early in childhood, stripped away not just by the adult world but by other children. In closing the essay *The Lost Childhood*, Greene quotes from the poem *Germinal* by A.E. Housman:

> In the lost boyhood of Judas
> Christ was betrayed.

Greene's feelings about betrayal were deep and individual. In 1968, he wrote of Kim Philby, the notorious senior officer in British Intelligence who was a double agent working for the Soviets for many years and who escaped to Russia in 1963:

> 'He betrayed his country' – yes, perhaps he did, but who among us has not committed treason to something or someone more important than a country?

Philby had been the boss of Burgess and Maclean, the MI6 agents who fled to Russia in 1951, hours before they were to be arrested as Soviet double agents. There was frequent speculation in the 1950s about who, inside the intelligence service, had alerted them to imminent exposure. This hidden traitor was universally dubbed *the third man* by the press. Twelve years later Philby (also escaping in the nick of time) was revealed as *the third man*. Subsequently he was acknowledged by the KGB as the most successful Soviet agent in post-war history.

By eerie coincidence, Philby had also been Greene's boss during his time as an agent in the war years. Greene had not only respected Philby for his intelligence work against the Germans at that time but also liked him, and continued to admire many of the man's personal qualities.

ideologies

contexts

post-war depression

SHADOWS OF WAR

The Vienna of *The Third Man* lived in the shadows of two wars, the Second World War and the Cold War: the first had been a disaster for its people, the second would carry the threat of catastrophe: Vienna was on the frontier of the Soviet empire and the West.

Many millions of people had died violently in the Second World War, the vast majority in Eastern Europe and Russia. The Russians captured Vienna (then part of the Third Reich) from the Germans in 1945. The fighting and destruction had been savage, as in all parts of the Eastern Front. The civilian population suffered very badly. About a quarter of all the buildings in Vienna were partly or completely destroyed, partly by American bombing, partly by Red Army artillery.

In 1948, three years after the end of the war – the year of the filming of *The Third Man* – Austria was still under military occupation, and would remain so for another seven years. The country was divided into four occupied zones, each controlled by one of the victorious allies, Soviet Russia, Britain, the USA and France.

By 1948, although the long task of reconstruction was well under way, the aftermath of war was strikingly visible in the city. For many of its people life was hard. Poverty, disease, hunger and crime were still widespread.

The Allies had created an international military police patrol for Vienna's inner city, The Austrians retained their civil police (including the Underground Police who patrol the city's enormous sewer system and who are seen dramatically in that task in the film), but they were subject to the command structure of the armies of occupation. The Allied military occupation provided law and justice of a sort in the city, but the alien presence added to the unhappiness of a defeated population.

The Vienna shown in *The Third Man* was still in the grip of post-war depression, the shattering of old certainties, a confusion of values which contribute to the elusive 'atmosphere' of the film.

The air of almost permanent military occupation in Vienna in 1948, with little sign of peace or 'normality', was one symptom of the Cold War between Soviet Russia and the West, then in its early days. The Cold War was deadly enmity without open warfare: two huge armies, heavily armed

contexts **cultural**

film 'treatment'

and ready for immediate action, threatening each other and the world with thermonuclear extinction.

Tensions between the Western and the Soviet governments on numerous issues increased steadily after the defeat of Germany in 1945. In 1948 the Russian blockaded West Berlin and in doing so marked the start of the Cold War. In reply, the West organised a huge airlift to supply the besieged city. Eleven months later, when *The Third Man* opened in London in 1949, the daily airlift to Berlin was still flying. With the formation of NATO in 1949, the Cold War started to assume its frightening air of permanence.

Vienna, like Berlin, a frontier between the East and West, was full of tensions, international dirty tricks and espionage in 1948. The fictional attempt by the Russian military to deport Anna to Czechoslovakia (part of the Eastern 'bloc') had its origins in many successful Russian kidnappings and deportations of refugees.

cultural

FILM AND NOVEL

Greene published his original story (the film 'treatment', first stage of the screenplay) of *The Third Man* in 1950, the year after the release of the film. He called it an 'Entertainment', the term he used for *Stamboul Train*, *A Gun for Sale* and other 'thrillers'. In his contract with London Films, Greene had retained the copyright of the 'treatment', a rare achievement for a writer.

At less than 120 pages, the book is really a novella – a long short story. Greene kept it short, as it was written solely with the imminent screenplay in mind. Years later, he said:

> I think one thing is certain: that a short story makes a much better film than a novel. A novel is too long. There is too much material. There have to be too many compromises. The cuts may seem unimportant but you suddenly find that an unimportant cut has changed the whole character of a character.

The success of the film lends support to this view. *The Third Man* was Greene's only original work for the cinema.

cultural contexts

book lacks film's excitement

The cinematic novel

The book of *The Third Man* has many of the virtues of the film: crisp dialogue, swift scene changes, and the plot is more convincing as a thriller than others of his 'Entertainments'. The word 'cinematic' has been used frequently about Greene's style in fiction; and the author was not unhappy with the term:

> GREENE: ... I've been mixed up with films for a very, very long time ... But it obviously influenced my writing.
>
> AUDIENCE: Could you mention something about the effect of the invention of the cinema on the technique of novel writing, from the point of view of the modern novelist?
>
> GREENE: Speaking for myself I think it means that, for instance in a description, one uses a moving camera instead of a stationary one. That description is part of the movement of a story and not a paragraph inserted as a stationary thing in a novel.
>
> Guardian Film Lecture, NFT, September 1984

The novel may disappoint many who enjoyed the film. The story, characters, and themes are very close and much of the dialogue recurs in the film, but the book lacks the excitement and 'atmosphere' of the film. Greene would probably have agreed. In the preface to *The Third Man* he wrote:

> The film, in fact, is better than the story because it is in this case the finished state of the story.

We know that the novel ended differently from the film. Some of the other differences between the novel and the film text are:

■ The narrator in the novel is Calloway, a less satisfying device than the detached point of view of the film text.

■ The tensions of Cold War politics are more elaborate in the book (particularly the subplot of the Russian attempt to kidnap Anna and repatriate her).

■ The Englishmen Rollo and Lime became the Americans Holly and Lime.

contexts — **cultural** influences

■ Lime's Romanian 'colleague' Popescu was originally US Army Colonel Cooler. Greene and Reed decided, perhaps in response to Selznick, that as Lime was now American, one American villain was enough.

INTERTEXTUALITY

The Third Man is an original film. Unclassifiable, it is hard to find comparators. But all films and books have, of course, been influenced by other films and books, as well as by much else. We have noted some of the influences on Reed's film style in *The Third Man* and seen the consistencies in the story and dialogue with the 'Greeneland' of Graham Greene's other work. Apart from these influences, the intertextuality of two, possibly three, other features needs to be considered.

The plot

Philip French has speculated that the plot of *The Third Man* might have been borrowed by Greene from Eric Ambler's *Mask of Dimitrios*. Both thrillers depend in part on the surprise of the 'dead protagonist who turns out not to be dead'. But this has been a not uncommon device in the plots of drama and fiction for hundreds of years. Readers of Ambler's book (or film), viewers of *The Third Man*, will find little otherwise remotely similar in the story, style or atmosphere of the two tales.

Laura (1944), a stylish 'noir' thriller, also has an undead protagonist. *Ride the Pink Horse* (1947), an unmemorable film by Robert Montgomery, has an ex-serviceman searching for the killer of his dead friend, as well as a crucial meeting in a fairground. Neither of these comes to mind even faintly when we watch *The Third Man*.

The interlude

The incident at the Cultural Centre, which provides a much-needed break from the tension of Holly's involvement with Lime's criminal friends, is both startling and funny. Holly's literary ordeal is a knowing tribute to Hitchcock's version of John Buchan's novel, *The Thirty Nine Steps* (1935), in which Hannay, the hero on the run, is mistaken for a political candidate and has to field voters' questions at a large meeting.

cultural contexts

allusions

The screenplay shows that in early drafts Greene's original character of Crabbin was expanded into two dim army officers, and the farce of mistaken identity was more prolonged. Reed had originally thought of recruiting to those roles the silly-ass duo of Basil Radford and Naunton Wayne, following their success in Hitchcock's *The Lady Vanishes* (1938) and Reed's *Night Train to Munich* (1940).

Mercifully, he had second thoughts: the episode was reduced severely and the two roles became one again. *The Third Man* could not have borne the prolonged jokiness of an English 'comedy-thriller'; and one brief Hitchcock reference was enough. Reed's interlude is shorter, funnier and closer to the action than Hitchcock's.

The title

Selznick thought that no one would want to go to see a film with a dull title like *The Third Man*.

The 'third man' of the title refers simply to the unknown man who is seen by the porter with Kurz and Popescu, carrying the 'body' of Lime across the street. But there are resonances, which may or may not have occurred to Greene when he chose the phrase.

Christopher Driver has suggested that the title might be a cynical allusion to the mysterious figure of the resurrected Christ who, in the Gospels, joins two of his disciples briefly on the road to Emmaeus.

Another, stronger possibility (Greene admired the poem very much) is that the title carries an allusion to the line in T.S. Eliot's *The Waste Land* – 'Who is the third who walks always beside you?'.

This line is itself a conscious reference to an episode related in Shackleton's Antarctic diary:

> I know that during that long and racking march of thirty six hours over the unnamed mountains and glaciers of South Georgia it seemed to me often that we were four, not three. I said nothing to my companions on the point, but afterwards Worsley said to me, 'Boss, I had a curious feeling on the march that there was another person with us'. Crean confessed to the same idea.

contexts   # cinematic

film noir?

Whatever the sources, the title of *The Third Man* continues to resonate eerily down the years.

cinematic

What of the film and its director in the context of cinematic history?

As a drama and thriller, *The Third Man* belongs to no *genre*, no formula. It has, at first, a resemblance in structure to the private-eye genre and style (friend turns investigator to find out truth of friend's death). But, as we have seen, the narrative shifts steadily into drama of a different kind.

The fact that Holly is himself a writer of *genre* – formulaic Western novels – is used mockingly in the film to illustrate the absurdity of his stance in a world he cannot understand:

```
HOLLY: The story's about a rider who hunted down a
sheriff who was victimising his best friend.
CRABBIN: Sounds exciting.
HOLLY: It is. I'm gunning just the same way for
your Major Callaghan.
```

and

```
CALLOWAY furious: I told you to go away, Martins.
This isn't Santa Fe, I'm not a sheriff, and you
aren't a cowboy ...
```

FILM NOIR?

French critics started to use the term 'noir' in the 1950s: more as a style than a genre. They had perceived a trend in Hollywood feature and 'B' films, a style and content matching that of hardboiled crime pulp fiction. (The generic term for these paperbacks in France was 'noir' because of the distinguishing colour of their covers.) These were tough, laconic, urban stories of crime and intrigue: murder and violence were commonplace; trust, loyalty, love were tested severely. Most endings were unhappy. Dashiell Hammett, James M. Cain, Raymond Chandler were at the high quality edge of the pulp detective fiction scene.

cinematic — contexts

expressionist use of angles

'I've just seen a dead man walking'

84   THE THIRD MAN

contexts   cinematic

Reed's films

In the style of *The Third Man* there are elements similar to that of many films which have been referred to loosely as 'noir'. If the *chiaroscuro* presentation of the night streets of Vienna and the expressionistic use of angles are evocative of early German cinema, they also remind us of the look and feel of certain Hollywood films of the forties: *Double Indemnity* (Billy Wilder), *The Woman in the Window* (Fritz Lang), *Dr Broadway* (Anthony Mann) and numerous others.

Is *The Third Man,* then, a film noir? Perhaps yes, perhaps no: it is debatable. Whatever our conclusion, it seems unlikely to add much to our knowledge of the film or judgement of its merits.

REED'S FILMS

In all, Carol Reed directed thirty-one films. In Background, we noted something of his apprenticeship years. Here we glance at a selection of the mature films by which he deserves to be remembered.

The Stars Look Down (1939) a social drama of the coal mines, adapted from A.J. Cronin's novel, starred Michael Redgrave as a young MP, a miner's son using his education in an attempt to reform the industry. The film is a vivid documentary-style portrait of a mining community and an inevitable colliery disaster, marred by an unconvincing romantic subplot.

Odd Man Out (1946) adapted from F.L. Green's novel, is a melodrama with the young James Mason as Johnny, a wounded IRA gunman, struggling on foot across Belfast from one alien hiding place to another to reach safety, and ends with his death. The film is distinguished by its fast pace, brilliant camerawork, editing, and its striking evocation of the nightmarish moods of a city. The style was exciting and disturbing, new to British cinema at the time.

The Fallen Idol (1948) was Reed's first film for Korda's London Films. It depicts brilliantly a child's innocence adrift in a small, flawed adult world, in this case an innocence which destroys that which it is trying to protect. A variation of this concern was to become apparent in *The Third Man*.

The Fallen Idol, adapted by Greene from his short story *The Basement Room*, is about Phil, a lonely small boy, the son of an ambassador, who

cinematic contexts

Reed's achievement

unwittingly incriminates his best friend, the butler Baines (Ralph Richardson), in the accidental death of his shrewish wife. Reed's empathy and patient skill brought out a compelling performance by the seven-year-old Bobby Henrey, totally convincing in the all-important role. The performances, camera-work and editing are all remarkable.

The Third Man (1949) is judged by most critics, and by popular choice, to be Reed's greatest work. But there are other claimants. Robert Moss in his thoughtful study of Reed's work argues cogently for *Odd Man Out* as 'Reed's masterpiece'.

Reed made three more films for Korda. Of these, only *An Outcast of the Islands* (1951) stands comparison with the three previous films. Generally regarded as a worthy failure (Conrad's intense psychological story of degradation may just be unfilmable) and certainly not a box-office success, *Outcast* was magnificently acted (Trevor Howard and Ralph Richardson) and visually compelling. Pauline Kael found it: 'one of the most unattended and underrated modern films'.

Later career

Following Korda's death in 1956, and the low state of the British film industry, Reed turned to Hollywood, seeking a platform for big-budget films. He made *Trapeze* (1956), brilliantly staged and shot, the action spectacular. But the story was trite, the characters stereotypical. It established Reed as a bankable director in the eyes of Hollywood.

Our Man in Havana (1959), despite the screenplay by Graham Greene, proved disappointing. The almost brutal switches between spy spoof comedy and personal tragedy do not work well on the screen.

Of the other eight films Reed made between 1950 and 1971, only the musical *Oliver!* (1968) achieved great popular and warm critical success. The film had spectacle, pace and craftsmanship familiar from his great days. What it did not have was the realism or the drama of individuals grappling with modern life that mark his best films.

Reed's achievement

For a number of years in the 1940s and 1950s, Reed's reputation was as high in Britain and in America as that of Hitchcock or of David Lean.

contexts — influence

impact on popular imagination

Mystifyingly, Reed's reputation as director steadily disappeared from view during the 1980s and 1990s. At the start of the new millennium it almost seems that he is remembered only for *The Third Man*.

Reed was not an innovator in the sense of finding a new approach to film narrative or devising new stylistic techniques. He was not an auteur: he did not originate stories. Most of his films are adaptations of novels.

An obsessive student of the art of film-making, Reed prepared minutely, drew on a wide range of techniques, and was a meticulous judge of how to use them to translate his vision on to film. His originality was in the way he *saw* the story and used the tools most fitting to present that vision.

It has been said disparagingly that Reed as a director was merely a craftsman. Modest always about his work, Reed might have agreed; but the evidence on screen in his best films reveals a master of narrative and style. A strong humanism, a wry sympathy for the beleaguered individual – the orphan, the fool, the outcast – coloured by a strong sense of realism and irony – mark his best work.

It is hard to avoid the conclusion that after Korda's death he lost his way in the harsh world of Hollywood. For the films he made in England, he had been able to select the story, actors and crew. Ironically for a director who believed that 'the really essential thing is a good script', Reed appears in his Hollywood years either to have lost his judgement in the selection of stories; or, more likely, was obliged to accept stories chosen by others.

influence

The Third Man has certainly made an impact on the popular imagination in the fifty years of its life.

The film was a box-office hit in 1949 and 1950 in the UK. For Korda it was a much-needed, very profitable release in Britain and in Europe. Sales figures are now unobtainable, but Selznick estimated that the USA gross would be between $6–$8 million, a high return for the period.

In July 1999, the fully restored print of *The Third Man* was released in the UK (to only three cinema screens in the country at any one time); and by

influence

contexts

instant popularity of zither music

Christmas 1999 takings had exceeded £200,000. The distributors, Optimum Releasing, described this as a 'phenomenal' success in today's terms.

ZITHER FEVER

Korda and Reed were astounded by the instant runaway popularity of the zither music of *The Third Man*. It was a huge hit, a maddening full-scale 'craze' that swept the country.

Demand from the public, from the radio, from the sheet music industry, started from the first day of the film's release. Anton Karas, recalled from Vienna, was offered fifty per cent of London Films' proceeds from the sale of records and sheet music. He made a studio recording (two sides of a 78 rpm disc: *The Harry Lime Theme* and *Café Mozart Waltz*).

The record was hurriedly released by Decca at the end of October 1949. After one month, the disc had sold half a million copies in the UK. Record charts did not exist at the time, but it is said that sales exceeded five million copies within three months. Dance bands everywhere were playing transcriptions. *The Harry Lime Theme* was, at the time, the biggest ever British popular music hit.

When the film opened in America in 1950, Selznick shamelessly headlined the cinema posters 'He'll have you in a dither with his zither'. The infection caught, the craze was repeated in America. This was something unique in the history of film-making. When we see the film, the zither music is impressive, immediately *right* as *part* of the film text. But listen to the music on its own, and it is impossible now to imagine why or how these simple sounds swept the western world like a fever in 1949 and 1950.

SPIN-OFFS

The impact of the film was strong and enduring. The fascination with Harry Lime lingered long after the 1949 release. In America in 1951–52, Welles performed in a radio series of more than fifty half-hour episodes, *The Lives of Harry Lime*. Lime rapidly became a sort of Robin Hood, an amiable, cynical international con-man and thief, his adventures damaging only to people much more unpleasant than he. Later, in 1959, Michael Rennie played Lime as a kind of international private eye in a

contexts   influence

references in fiction and media

television series which enjoyed a moderate success. These poor spin-offs have all but disappeared from public memory.

CULT OR MYTH?

Evidence persists down the years of admirers, fans, devotees of the film, across generations and national boundaries. References to the story, to Harry Lime, to lines of dialogue, keep surfacing fifty years later, in fiction, journalism, the media, even casually between strangers. Speaking of a visit to the great Wheel in Vienna in 1998, Charles Drazin reports:

> As we clanked to a halt just short of the two-hundred-foot-high summit, a Japanese tourist said in English, 'Flee of income tax, old man. Flee of income tax'. He stuck his camcorder out of the window, pointing it down towards the ground …

Is *The Third Man* a cult? 'Cult' is probably too strong a word, but 'myth' might be appropriate:

> When we look for a myth of the times, we might consider whether *The Third Man* doesn't offer more than acceptably lofty works like *The Waste Land* or *Doctor Faustus* or *The Magic Mountain*. It has reached more people, and having reached them, held them in its irresistible narrative spell.
>
> Paul Driver, A Third Man Cento

Or this, from an American thriller in 1999, one example of many passing references in fiction and the media:

> 'He said no adult in the postwar world had the right to be as innocent as Holly Martens was.' … He looked back at me. 'You agree, Mr Detective?'
> I nodded. 'I always thought Calloway was the only hero in that movie.'
> He snapped his fingers. 'Trevor Howard. Me, too'. He looked up at his wife …
>
> Dennis Lehane, Prayers for Rain

evaluation   contexts

evaluation

Critical response to *The Third Man* has developed during the half century of its life.

British critics were excited by *The Third Man* on its first release in 1949; but there was an undercurrent of disappointment. Reed's bravura display of technique worried several of those who had admired his innovations in the past. Perhaps content had been sacrificed to style?

> There are passages in the Reed-Greene film with a touch of the pretentiousness which creeps into the later Welles films ... To say all this is, I know, to be hypercritical. But *The Third Man* is excellent enough to be judged by severe standards.
>
> Dilys Powell, The Sunday Times

Sight and Sound gave a measured welcome to the film in 1949:

> By the very nature of its settings and story, there are occasional reminiscences of Lang and Hitchcock, but there is nothing borrowed or imitated. Stylistically, *The Third Man* is Reed's most impressive film ... as an analyst of mood and situation, Reed is practically unequalled today ...
>
> GL, Monthly Film Bulletin, September 1949

Most American critics were impressed when the film opened in the USA five months later, but there was some dissent. Was this just an example of great craftsmanship applied to a routine thriller?

John McCurten writing in *The New Yorker* was perhaps the most dismissive of any critic on either side of the Atlantic:

> Mr Reed in this one has frequently permitted the action to slow down to a saunter, and has indulged, I'm afraid, entirely too much in trick camera angles to nudge along laggard episodes.

Bosley Crowther in *The New York Times* thought the story 'just a bang-up melodrama, designed to excite and entertain'. But, he went on:

contexts — evaluation

status of a 'classic'

> Mr Reed has brilliantly packaged the whole bag of his cinematic tricks, his whole range of inventive genius for making the camera expound. His eminent gifts for compressing a wealth of suggestion in single shots, for building up agonised tension and popping surprises are fully exercised ...

MID-TERM REVIEWS

As the years passed, *The Third Man* steadily acquired the status of a 'classic' film, recurringly popular with mass audiences on television, constantly sought by enthusiasts in film societies.

By the end of the 1980s, a number of analytical and reflective articles on *The Third Man* had been published in journals, and the tone had become more appreciative of content as well as style. The themes of the story, the subtext of the thriller, were now seen to be more important as part of the film's success than they had appeared in 1949.

As the 1990s opened, *Sight and Sound* published a remarkable reading of *The Third Man*, illuminating with detailed attention the contribution of about twenty scenes:

> It is a rare example of popular art achieving transcendence; a thriller embracing the most serious themes; a powerful statement about the nature of love and evil, about the depravity and shattered beauty of our century ... Reed arrives at full mastery of the medium in this film ... in which well-madeness is raised to the level of genius – and the poignancy of the results is unsurpassed.
>
> *Paul Driver, A Third Man Cento*

Four years later, also in *Sight and Sound* (April, 1994), Philip Kemp wrote a retrospective review of *The Third Man*, emphasising its textual unity:

> Every element – people, place, subject matter – seems to have come together in one flawless, pre-ordained package ... In *The Third Man*, melodrama attains sublimity. Welles' playing of the Prater Wheel scene conveys, behind its surface jauntiness, a sense of that same horror – the emptiness of the moral abyss.

evaluation — contexts

top of the list

MILLENNIAL REVIEWS

The restored print of *The Third Man* was released in 1999, first in the USA and then in Britain. In the press, critical enthusiasm was strong, apparently unanimous. The subtext was again more to the fore than in 1949; and the style still fascinated after fifty years:

> *The Third Man* captures in amber a brief, poignant moment of postwar history – the partitioned, romantic Vienna – yet remains timeless in its wit, sophistication, excitement and complex morality.
>
> *Philip French, The Observer*

PRIZES AND POLLS

Awards: *The Third Man* won the Palme d'Or (Best Film) at the Cannes Film Festival 1949. Robert Krasker's cinematography won him the Academy Award for black and white cinematography in 1951. Carol Reed had been nominated, but it was not until 1968 that he won the award for best director, for the now largely forgotten musical *Oliver!*

The AFI poll: In June 1999, the American Film Institute announced its list of the one hundred greatest American Movies ('all produced during the first hundred years of American film-making'). *The Third Man* was fifty-seventh in the list (between *MASH* and *Fantasia*). It is curious (perhaps flattering) that *The Third Man* was seen as an American movie.

The BFI poll: In September 1999, the British Film Institute published the results of its poll of 'one thousand people embracing all strands of the film, cinema and television industries throughout the UK' to find the 'culturally British feature films of the 20th century, which they felt had made a strong and lasting impression'. Of a shortlist of a hundred films *The Third Man* emerged top of the list.

FILM STUDIES

Despite the admiration of the industry, the public and reviewers, Carol Reed appears to be out of fashion today in much of the British academic world of film studies. If one can judge by standard reference works, Reed seems to have been erased from history. For example, there is no mention at all of *The Third Man*, or of Reed and his films, in the 600 pages of *The Oxford Guide to Film Studies*, 1998 ('comprehensive, authoritative and unique') or in the 500 pages of the Routledge *Introduction to Film Studies* (a 'comprehensive textbook for students of cinema').

OVERVIEW

The Third Man can be judged as a work of art and as a work of entertainment, for it is both; and the boundary between the two is blurred. Reed and Greene were alike in their strong rejection of any notion that art should serve a social purpose. Their intention was to entertain: their instincts and talents were artistic and individual.

The Third Man has exercised a fascination for very many: a desire to see it again, to reflect on it and to refer to it. Time has not dimmed its appeal. The story, the characters, their actions, their motives are not outmoded, and never will be. Despite enormous changes in the world and in society, these are recognisably 'modern' men and women. The themes of the film, the dilemmas of love and betrayal, the seductiveness of evil, the hard choices of survival in the urban jungle, still give us pause. The values persist. The thriller still grips, the style enchants.

Durability, time's test of the market over a long period, is in the end the only reliable yardstick of the value of a work of art or of entertainment. After fifty years, *The Third Man* has so far survived that test brilliantly; its prospects in the new millennium are promising.

bibliography

Altman – Nowell-Smith

general film

Altman, Rick, *Film Genre*, BFI, 1999
　Detailed exploration of film genres

Bordwell, David, *Narration in the Fiction Film*, Routledge, 1985
　A detailed study of narrative theory and structures

– – –, Staiger, Janet & Thompson, Kristin, *The Classical Hollywood Cinema: Film Style & Mode of Production to 1960*, Routledge, 1985; pbk 1995
　An authoritative study of cinema as institution, it covers film style and production

– – – & Thompson, Kristin, *Film Art*, McGraw-Hill, 4th edn, 1993
　An introduction to film aesthetics for the non-specialist

Branson, Gill & Stafford, Roy, *The Media Studies Handbook*, Routledge, 1996

Buckland, Warren, *Teach Yourself Film Studies*, Hodder & Stoughton, 1998
　Very accessible, it gives an overview of key areas in film studies

Cook, Pam (ed.), *The Cinema Book*, BFI, 1994

Corrigan, Tim, *A Short Guide To Writing About Film*, HarperCollins, 1994
　What it says: a practical guide for students

Dyer, Richard, *Stars*, BFI, 1979; pbk Indiana University Press, 1998
　A good introduction to the star system

Easthope, Antony, *Classical Film Theory*, Longman, 1993
　A clear overview of recent writing about film theory

Hayward, Susan, *Key Concepts in Cinema Studies*, Routledge, 1996

Hill, John & Gibson, Pamela Church (eds), *The Oxford Guide to Film Studies*, Oxford University Press, 1998
　Wide-ranging standard guide

Lapsley, Robert & Westlake, Michael, *Film Theory: An Introduction*, Manchester University Press, 1994

Maltby, Richard & Craven, Ian, *Hollywood Cinema*, Blackwell, 1995
　A comprehensive work on the Hollywood industry and its products

Mulvey, Laura, 'Visual Pleasure and Narrative Cinema' (1974), in *Visual and Other Pleasures*, Indiana University Press, Bloomington, 1989
　The classic analysis of 'the look' and 'the male gaze' in Hollywood cinema. Also available in numerous other edited collections

Nelmes, Jill (ed.), *Introduction to Film Studies*, Routledge, 1996
　Deals with several national cinemas and key concepts in film study

Nowell-Smith, Geoffrey (ed.), *The Oxford History of World Cinema*, Oxford University Press, 1996
　Hugely detailed and wide-ranging with many features on 'stars'

bibliography

the third man

Thomson – Wapshott

Thomson, David, *A Biographical Dictionary of the Cinema*, Secker & Warburg, 1975
  Unashamedly driven by personal taste, but often stimulating

Truffaut, François, *Hitchcock*, Simon & Schuster, 1966, rev. edn, Touchstone, 1985
  Landmark extended interview

Turner, Graeme, *Film as Social Practice*, 2nd edn, Routledge, 1993
  Chapter four, 'Film Narrative', discusses structuralist theories of narrative

Wollen, Peter, *Signs and Meaning in the Cinema*, Viking, 1972
  An important study in semiology

Readers should also explore the many relevant websites and journals. *Film Education* and *Sight and Sound* are standard reading.

Valuable websites include:

The Internet Movie Database at http://uk.imdb.com

Screensite at http://www.tcf.ua.edu/screensite/contents.html

The Media and Communications Site at the University of Aberystwyth at http://www.aber.ac.uk/~dgc/welcome.html

There are obviously many other university and studio websites which are worth exploring in relation to film studies.

the third man

Drazin, Charles, *In Search of The Third Man*, Methuen, 1999
  New revelations and speculation about the background and making of the film, expertly researched

Greene, Graham, *The Third Man* (screenplay), Faber and Faber, 1988
  Script endorsed by Greene and Reed. The progress of the 'final' three drafts of the screenplay can be followed

Greene, Graham, *The Third Man* (novel), Penguin, 1997
  An 'Entertainment', Greene's original 'treatment' for the film

Greene, Graham, *Ways of Escape*, Bodley Head, 1980
  Includes Greene's views on Selznick

Moss, Robert F. *The Films of Carol Reed*, Columbia University Press, New York, 1987
  A fine account of Reed's films and career: it may be the only monograph on Reed currently in print

Parkinson, David (ed), *The Graham Greene Film Reader*, Carcanet Press, London, 1994
  Treasurehouse of Greene's writing for and about the cinema: irresistible

Sherry, Norman, *The Life of Graham Greene*, Jonathan Cape, 1994
  This long, absorbing biography (two volumes, the third imminent) is likely to be the definitive 'life'

Stratford, Philip (ed), *The Portable Graham Greene*, Penguin, 1994
  Selection of Greene's fiction and non-fiction

Wapshott, Nicholas, *The Man Between*, Chatto & Windus, 1990
  A revealing biography of Carol Reed

credits

production
Alexander Korda, David O. Selznick, London Films

produced and directed by
Carol Reed

original story and screenplay by
Graham Greene

music composed and played by
Anton Karas

associate producer
Hugh Perceval

production manager
T.S. Lyndon-Haynes

art director
Vincent Korda

assistant art directors
John Hawkesworth, Joseph Bato

director of photography
Robert Krasker

edited by
Oswald Hafenrichter

camera operators
Edward Scaife, Denys Coop

additional photography by
John Wilcox, Stan Pavey

sound
John Cox

length
9,428 ft

time
1 hour 44 minutes

shot
At the London Film Studios, Shepperton, England, and on location in Austria

cast
Holly Martins – Joseph Cotten
Anna – Alida Valli
Harry Lime – Orson Welles
Major Calloway – Trevor Howard
Sergeant Paine – Bernard Lee
Porter – Paul Hoerbiger
Porter's wife – Annie Rosar
'Baron' Kurz – Ernst Deutsch
Popescu – Siegfried Breuer
Dr Winkel – Erich Ponto
Crabbin – Wilfrid Hyde-White
Anna's landlady – Hedwig Bleibtrau
Hansl – Herbert Halbik
Brodsky – Alexis Chesnakov
Hall porter at Sacher's – Paul Hardtmuth